Don't Be Denied

Your

Authority

by Stan Riley

Joy Publishing

P.O. Box 9901
Fountain Valley, CA 92708
www.joypublishing.com

Don't Be Denied

Your

Authority

by Stan Riley

© 2000 Stan Riley 2nd Edition

Published by: Joy Publishing
P.O. Box 9901
Fountain Valley, CA 92708
www.joypublishing.com

ISBN 0-939513-38-2

Printed in the United States of America

The King James Version of the Holy Bible has been used unless noted otherwise.

Table of Contents

Stan's sayings,

You won't learn anything new until you come into conflict with what you already know.

Increase your faith by using it.

We must be silent to hear.

Stop depending on "stuff."

Demons fear the devil
more than Christians fear God.

Passivity is not faith.

Instead of looking at ourself and saying,
"I can't do it," look at Him and say,
"He can, so I can."

We might just as well profit from the mistakes of others. We probably won't live long enough to make all of them ourselves.

A Note of Thanks

First, I thank God who has chosen me, a shy and introverted person, and made me His own child. He took me from a promising secular career and thrust me into full-time ministry for 37 years. He gave me my own non-denominational church, Mountain Fellowship of Prescott, Arizona, and a throng of people to minister to. In these last seven years, now that I thought I could retire, He has seen fit to keep on using me.

Thanks to my wife, Marilee, for all the long hours of study, research, and writing that has gone into this new book. She is an amazing woman.

I owe a big debt of thanks to my publisher Woody Young. He had the courage to take on my first book. At that time few people understood the impact of it; however, he believed in this message and has faithfully spread the word. Every few months he has invited Marilee and me to be his house guests and speak to people who are seeking. As a result of the questions raised in some of these seminars, we were challenged to write this new book. A businessman with worldwide responsibilities, Woody has continued to be a blessing to the Lord's work.

Thanks to my friends, Don and Elaine Hardt, for their encouragement. They demanded that I come all this year, once a week to their home, and let them glean out of me what the Lord had taught me and was still teaching me. They handed out dozens of copies of *Don't Be Denied God's Power*. They invited pastors and other believers to come, listen, and ask questions. Elaine has edited this book, adding her journalistic skills to make sure that all the points are well presented.

Thanks also to all of my family and friends. You've kept me on my toes with your questions. You've put up with my jokes. You've invited me to your homes to minister to your friends. You've prayed for me.

And thanks to YOU for reading this book. Pass it on.

"But covet earnestly the best gifts . . ." (1 Corinthians 12:31).

To Pastors Only

Some of us have the feeling that we're not quite making it spiritually. What we have been doing and what we think will work has not. We want to do better.

We think prayer will make the difference. We have prayed. It has not.

We think reading the Bible will make the difference. We did. It has not.

What's going on?

Dear brothers, please read this book with an open heart. God has called you to a difficult and serious job, shepherding the flock. I understand the pressures you are under, the unreasonable expectations you may face.

I want you to know how precious you are to God.

Above all else, I want to encourage and bless you with this message of power and authority.

You will be judged more than the ordinary man in the pew. Are you doing what God wants? Are you preaching boldly? Are you discipling your people?

Perhaps your denomination calls these truths by a different term or has a different cultural tradition. Perhaps you fear for your job if you step out and take your stand for the Bible's truth.

You must weigh your options: Continue and be less of a man than you could be? Keep on being a man-pleaser? Or, be honest before God and cry out and repent? He will give you a new beginning as you allow Him to give you more power and authority.

Take what He is giving. Do what He is saying.

With great respect and with great audacity,

A fellow pastor, Stan Riley

Read This First

I want you to read this book. It continues the important message of my previous book, *Don't Be Denied God's Power.* Now I want you to learn this: *Don't Be Denied Your Authority.*

Power and authority—that's what the Christian life is all about.

I've learned more.
Since the book on power was published, people have urged me to continue writing. Each new experience with healing and freeing people from the stranglehold of the devil has taught me more about God--about His power and the authority He wants us to have.

I've seen more miracles.
I have seen more insane adults and children become whole right before my very eyes. I have seen more cancer and other deadly diseases dissipate, to our fresh amazement once again. I have seen more occult-driven, frenzied neurotics made whole in their minds and sent home to their families with the good news.   I have seen more believers take on their "new" authority, and walk in a victory they didn't know could be theirs because they hadn't heard it before.

The authority we have is clearly stated.
The miraculous was not just a rare occurrence in the New Testament. God's people were *expecting* signs and wonders. The early church saw amazing things.

How can we turn aside from our Lord who said, *"If you love Me, keep My commandments"*? (John 14:15 and John 15:10). Again the believers were instructed to do so in 1 John 5:2,3.

There's a time to *PRAY*, and there's a time to *SAY*.

God has so much more for us, if we'll only take hold of it. We must learn when to pray about it and when to rise up with His authority and *say* it.

"Whosoever shall say unto this mountain, Be thou removed, and be thou cast into the sea; and shall not doubt in his heart, but shall believe that those things which he saith shall come to pass; he shall have whatsoever he saith." (Mark 11:23)

I had to write this book.

I knew it wasn't fair to keep this teaching to myself and my own circle of friends and local church family. So, gentle as God is with me, I know this book must be done. I claim 1 Thessalonians 5:24 which tells me that faithful is He who calls me, who will also do it.

I've made the Holy Spirit my best friend. He's taught me some new and better ways to minister to hurting and seeking people.

So I place these truths in your hands with the prayer that you allow His Holy Spirit to become your best friend. Allow Him to teach you about His power and your authority, and continually show you new truths and better strategies. Then, if you will, share with me what He has shown you, so that we might truly become together that beautifully obedient and powerful Bride He will be married to forever.

His servant, and yours,

Stan Riley
smriley@northlink.com

Note: I'm quoting from the *King James* version of the Bible. The numbers used refer to *Strong's Exhaustive Concordance*. I recommend both of these books to you. Dig in and find out.

Chapter **1**

God Gives Us His Authority

I've seen people healed of cancer, deadly heart conditions, even healed of 50 warts on the hands. I've seen people who were being tormented by evil spirits thrown across the room and bounced around like animals.

I've delivered a teen who was so messed up she was headed for a life of crime if she didn't commit suicide first.

I've seen hundreds of hurting people find the help they need. It all started over 30 years ago when I saw another man heal a desperately ill woman, and I told myself, "If he can do it, I can do it, too."

At that point, reading the Bible and praying took on a totally new dimension in my life. Ever since that first startling revelation from God I have been experiencing His power and authority daily as I minister to others.

What surprises me now is that more Christians aren't doing it. Why in the world do we think we're ordained to a life of ease? Perhaps some believers are confused from the teaching and example of others. Or, perhaps believers have not dealt with old, festering wounds in their own souls.

I have good news for you! God wants to give you the power and authority to do great and wonderful things.

In this book I'll show you how, by using the Scripture, to overcome incorrect teaching. I'll show you who you really are in Christ Jesus. I'll show you how to accept the gifts of the Spirit.

You have a calling from God, a special ministry to exercise. Something great that only you can do.

Is it risky? I call it exciting. I call it fulfilling.

Will you be misunderstood? Probably. What difference does it make, as long as you are doing what God has told you to do. All you need right now is a willingness to learn.

What is Authority?

Jesus, Himself, gave spectacular commands to His followers, along with the power and authority to do them. He gave us that same power and authority. He intended that those first followers pass His commands on to the next generation, and that generation to pass it along to the next, and so on. In this way the commands of Jesus come to us and are as binding upon us as they were to His first followers.

The Great Commission

> *Jesus came and spake unto them, saying, All power is given unto me in heaven and in earth. Go ye, therefore, and teach all nations, baptizing them in the name of the Father, and of the Son, and of the Holy Ghost, Teaching them to observe all things whatsoever I have commanded you; and, lo, I am with you always, even unto the end of the world. Amen.* (Matthew 28:18-20)

Notice that the word "observe" (#5083, *tereo*) means to keep, to attend to carefully. It implies to maintain; in other words, to continue doing all the things that Jesus had told them and taught them to do.

The Fivefold Commission:

> *And as ye go, preach, saying, The kingdom of heaven is at hand. Heal the sick, cleanse the lepers, raise the dead, cast out devils: freely ye have received, freely give.* (Matthew 10:7-8)

The Promise of the Power of the Holy Spirit

> *But ye shall receive power, after that the Holy Ghost is come upon you: and ye shall be*

witnesses unto me both in Jerusalem, and in all Judea, and in Samaria, and unto the uttermost part of the earth. (Acts 1:8)

Armed with the power of the indwelling Holy Spirit, and in obedience to the commands of Jesus, we may confidently use the authority God gives us.

Overcoming Fears with Authority

Read the newspapers, watch the news on television; things are bad now, and we're in for big trouble. The normal reaction would be fear. But bold believers see the mighty hand of God moving.

This book is about how to practice overcoming today so that we will be proficient at getting the victory over tomorrow's events, no matter *how* the Book of Revelation unfolds right under our noses.

Do I Have Enough Faith?

Don't get hung up on your uncertainty about having enough faith. The average Christian has been taught to seek and depend upon faith which leaves room for doubt, whereas dealing with the problems from the angle of Authority—to the extent of even having faith in ourselves—is a better approach.

We often think of faith from a hopeful standpoint. We realize we don't have enough faith; thus, we hope for and struggle to get more faith.

Authority can be visible. Like the foreman on the job who can hire and fire, we can picture authority. Jesus did not heal and deliver by His faith. He did it by authority. It's not that faith isn't important, but to do the works of God we need authority.

Incredible Trouble Is Coming in the World.

Today those familiar end-time scriptures seem to come alive in strangely new and unsettling ways as we match them up to the daily news. Wars, famines, floods, pestilence, and the downward economic spin of nations are not surprising God—and should not surprise us.

And the merchants of the earth shall weep and mourn over her; for no man buyeth their merchandise any more. (Revelation 18:11)

God Is in Control

The whole chapter of Revelation 18 is a wild account of worldwide economic ruin. Whether or not events will be exactly as the worldly predictors say is of no matter. The important part to remember is that launching into the twenty-first century, with its predictions of incredible changes, is going to require great understanding of what God both promises us and expects of us.

God prefaced all this in the earlier chapters of Revelation with the pictures of His true churches who are taught to "overcome," "overcome," "overcome."

(Revelation 2:7,11,17,25; 3:5,12,21) Overcome in the Greek is the word (#3528), *nikao*, which means "to get the victory over."

That's why this book is all about how to practice overcoming *now* so that we will be proficient at getting the victory over tomorrow's events, without the panic that will overtake the unprepared as Revelation unfolds. What the world needs to fear is the Second Coming of Christ.

We Need Not Fear the Future.

The angels told the shepherds in Bethlehem to "Fear not!" when they were surrounded and scared by the ominous new sights and sounds of a host of angels announcing the birth of Christ. Just so we are told in Revelation to "Fear not" at the sight of angels coming to do their awesome jobs at the Second Coming of Christ. (Revelation 1:17; 2:10)

Fear *not*? That seems a human impossibility.

How can we overcome and not be afraid in the light of such predictions? Because we are *promised* that God has given us everything we need to overcome evil—both that which is in us and that which surrounds us.

> *But evil men and seducers shall wax worse and worse, deceiving, and being deceived. But continue thou in the things which thou hast learned ...*
> (2 Timothy 3:13, 14)

Though evil is increasing more than ever as predicted, God would not ask us to do something that He has not already given us the ability to do. His promise is that He will show us how and provide the tools and skills with which to do them.

God's Promises Do Not Change

God has always promised to be *"a lamp unto our feet and a light unto our paths"* (Psalm 119:105) where none of us has gone yet, and where all of us are going together.

Why would these promises change just because we are now living in the end times? Each new generation has had different challenges, different dangers, different diseases than the generations before. But God has never changed, nor has His plan changed to make mankind into His collective, powerful Bride.

My calling has always been to call the church to become a perfected Bride. He is coming for a perfect Church. (Ephesians 4:12, 13). "Perfect" means "complete." Scripture is the tool with which He perfects His Church, and all pastors need to be used of God, especially at this end-time when there is no more time to fool around and be lukewarm. They are to teach the entire Word, not just bits and pieces. We are to use the Word of God to perfect those sheep He has entrusted to us.

All scripture is given by inspiration of God, and is profitable for doctrine, for reproof, for correction, for instruction in righteousness, That

n of God may be perfect, throughly
∂d unto all good works. (2 Timothy 3:16,17)

Come learn with me about the authority we have over our enemies, over our fears and other emotions, over our circumstances, over diseases, and over demonic activity.

Jesus Demonstrated Authority

Jesus said, "Go in my name." "Name" in the Greek is *onoma,* meaning character and authority. Learn with me how to live your life with Jesus' attitude, His character, and His authority.

His authority over fear (see Him fight fear in the Garden of Gethsemane). (Matthew 26:39)

His authority in the way He went around preaching boldly what His Father said, right in the faces of the tough Jewish Pharisees. (John 8:1-28)

His authority as He healed in accordance with what His Father said — against the will of the "religious right." (John 9:16)

His authority as He walked safely right through the middle of the angry crowd. (John 8:59).

The church as a whole doesn't have that kind of authority today. But we should, and we can. Why don't we? Because . . .

Confusion Has Made Us Weak

Instead of having authority, we've allowed ourselves to fall into the enemy's trap. We've permitted confusion to captivate our minds. We've ignored all the Scripture that tells us what to do and how to do it.

We have slipped into casually using clichés, such as "in the name of Jesus" and "we plead the blood" as if just saying so is going to get the job done. And then we wonder why we aren't as effective as the Word promises we will be. What is wrong? We have forgotten how to *use* His authority, instead of just saying His name! We have forgotten that "the power of the blood of Christ" has already washed us of our sins so that God's wrath is no longer against us. We're reciting words. We're in the rut of routine. We're hung up on traditions. We have gotten lazy!

This is no time to be lazy!

Read the bad news. There are new deadly diseases, new mental illnesses, longer-reaching warheads and technologies, more drastic economic crises. Violence and crime are epidemic.

Now read the Good News. These times require a new review of the Word, allowing God's Holy Spirit to work in us His awesome power and to give us His awesome authority. Read the end of the Book; we win!

You and I Can Be Overcomers

Let's turn the tide! Let's enter this twenty-first century and go to heaven as overcomers, with our heads held high and triumphant, victorious over our enemies, pleasing the Father, just as Jesus said.

These are exciting times. These are the times when *we* are going to watch God's promises come true right before *our* eyes. These times have been set up so that we refine our skills as *overcomers*. We are His Bride overcoming Christ's enemy with Him. We can be part of the cast of thousands who win with Him *if* we learn how to be the authority-empowered overcomers God has called us to be, with our foundation centered firmly on His Word.

Be Open to God's Word

Don't let God's Word slide off your mind like water off a duck's back. Ask the Holy Spirit to open the Word, teach you, correct you, and empower you with new understanding. Mix the Word with your faith. Don't be like the folks who missed out:

> *For unto us was the gospel preached, as well as unto them: but the word preached did not profit them, not being mixed with faith in them that heard it.* (Hebrews 4:2)

God is not looking for a denomination. He's looking for an individual. Don't wait until your denomination changes. Do what God shows *you* to do.

Chapter **2**

Authority From the Beginning

Someday you may find yourself in a tough situation. Someone may need help desperately—perhaps scriptural advice, healing, salvation, or deliverance.

Do you know a church where this person could get help right away, without delay?

Do you know anyone who could deal with the problem?

You need to be the one who can minister to this person. *You* need to be ready to speak healing, cast out tormenting spirits, pointing these people to Jesus for salvation.

You can do it—if you've learned ahead of time to not be denied your authority from God.

Jesus said some amazing things that many Christians don't yet believe, so most Christians cannot do them. You're going to hear the startling truth about the Great Commission and some almost unbelievable true stories from my own experience.

Get ready to have your understanding challenged and your beliefs stretched. Have your Bible at hand; check out every verse I give you. You are personally responsible for learning and doing what Jesus said.

I've been down this path myself and have grown immensely as I learned to make the Holy Spirit my best friend. He teaches and counsels me. Let Him be your best friend, too.

The Authority That Belongs to Believers

We are promised authority. Not the kind that the world has, which says *"I have the right to tell you what to do."* (Mark 10:42)

It's the kind of authority we are promised by God, from Genesis to Revelation. It has to do with first finding His will and then doing it boldly, but not arrogantly. It is what Jesus did when He taught or healed or delivered.

Jesus heard God's will and then did it. He heard how to heal, and He did it. He heard from His Father how to heal the sick, cleanse the lepers, raise the dead, and then He did it. This is His will for us: that we do the same. *"He that believes on me, the works that I do shall he do also."* (John 14:12)

Do you believe it? Do you have it? Do you want it? It was intended for us from the very beginning.

From the Beginning . . .

God's first command to man was *"to subdue"* and *"have authority over the fish of the sea, the fowl of the air and every living thing that moves upon the earth."* (Genesis 1:28) Plants, animals, and people are "living things;" so are germs and demons. Man was made to take care of and control the Earth's growth. We are to be like God, in His *"image,"* only under His supervision.

This command was repeated in the New Testament and called *"predestination."* From the beginning we were *"predestined to be conformed into the image of His Son,"* (Romans 8:29) It is the predestined reason for which we were created.

We were made to do as Jesus did, with His attitude. Jesus had great control, under his Father's close supervision, over His flesh, over His surrounding circumstances, over diseases, over angry crowds, over the weather and the sea.

The weather? Remember Elijah who was a *"man subject to like passions as we are, and he prayed earnestly that it might not rain; and it rained not on the earth by the space of three years and six months. And he prayed again, and the heaven gave rain, and the earth brought forth her fruit."* (James 5:17-18)

Jesus was an *over*comer. He had the authority to do whatever He heard the Father tell Him, and then He said we could do the same things. *"Verily, verily, I say unto you, He that believeth on me, the works that I do shall he do also; and greater [works] than these shall he do; because I go unto my Father."* (John 14:12)

Adam had this authority. Jesus had it. We are to have it. Once you catch hold of this truth in your spirit, you will notice it every time you pick up your Bible Let's look at it step by step.

Adam's Authority

Adam—the very first man God gave authority to—decided to use this God-given authority without God's control. God had told Adam that he was not to get the knowledge of good and evil from *"the tree of knowledge of good and evil."* (Genesis 2:16). God wanted man, instead, to always get that knowledge from Himself, as they talked in the Garden. He wanted a close-knit relationship with His creation, but He wanted to give him that choice. He did not want a robot.

He wanted someone He could love who would love Him back. A Bride. The kind of person who would choose and love Him as a Master and Friend, someone with whom He could have a relationship. We can't have a relationship with the Someone-who-knows-everything if we already think we can know it all and can make decisions without Him. So He set up a plan whereby mankind could choose to get their knowledge either from Him or from a tree.

This is spiritual death: "I don't need God because I can figure this out by myself." It is a choice to separate yourself from the Source of life who is God Himself. This is the original sin, and it's just as original today as it was then. It's your inherited tendency to want to figure out your circumstances without Him because you like being Lord of your own life.

Satan knew that mankind had been given that authority over the Earth. He wanted it for himself, however, so he tried to talk them out of it. He didn't go directly to Adam, because it was to Adam God had spoken about his authority. *"And God commanded the man, saying. . ."* (Genesis 2:16, emphasis added) So Satan waited until they were separated and Eve was alone. Now somewhere down the line, Adam must have told Eve what God had said about the tree because she repeated those instructions (not quite accurately) to Satan when he made her question herself as to whether she had authority or not. Listen to his subtle approach, as he tries to build doubt in her, the way he still does with us today.

The serpent asked her, *"Has God said, You should not eat of every tree of the garden"?"* (Genesis 3:1) The real question, asked clearly and honestly, should have been, "Did God say you couldn't eat of the tree of knowledge of good and evil?" That would have been more straightforward. But he was trying to entice her and get her to doubt exactly what God had said. She tried to think it through by herself. She should have called Adam, or God, or both, and said, "Hey, this serpent here is asking me a tricky question. Let's face this unusual fellow together." But no, she tried to quote the instructions alone. She said, *"We may eat of the fruit of the trees of the garden: but of the fruit of the tree which is in the midst of the garden, God has said, Ye shall not eat of it neither shall ye touch it lest you die."* (Genesis 3:2, 3)

Did God tell them not to *touch* the fruit? No. Satan knew she didn't have it quite right. So, seeing she was confused on one *little* point, he plugged away at her, and got her more confused, and she ate some. Sound familiar? Satan tries to talk us out of our God-given authority a little at a time. If he were to come and say, "God is not good, and He doesn't know everything," we would say, "Oh, bug off!" But he comes in, one sneaky little thought at a time, and subtly beguiles us.

By the time Adam came back into the picture, he too forgot to call on God to clarify this mess, and tried to figure it out without his Source of life and wisdom. Instead of using His God-given authority to say, "Be gone and leave my wife alone," he reasoned with his own finite brilliant mind.

Thus he, along with Eve, forfeited their right to rule the earth over to Satan. Satan was given the authority over the earth by the very ones to whom God had given it. God could not deny them this choice. Choosers must be free to choose. Adam, then, became Satan's servant for you truly do *become the servant of the one whom you obey.* (Romans 6:16)

For the next 2,000 years God allowed mankind to rule the Earth without this authority, to experience what it was like. The wickedness of men became so *"great in the earth that every imagination of the thought of his heart was only evil continually."* (Genesis 6:5) Only Noah, who "found grace in the eyes of the Lord," was an exception to this rule. If God had not saved him and the other seven members of his family, mankind would have annihilated itself and the whole wonderful plan for this planet would have been canceled out.

Abraham's Authority

In the year 2000 God found and chose a man named Abraham and promised him that through him and his descendants a Messiah (a God/Man) would come to buy back their right to rule the Earth again. God made a covenant with them, that He would save them and return their authority to them. If they, the Israelites, would believe that He would come one day, they could be His. If they did not believe that, they would not be His. Choices again.

This was the story of the next 2,000 years. Their stories fill the Old Testament from Genesis 12 to the last chapter, Malachi. Moses, David, Elijah, and the rest of those familiar prophets and kings all tried to regain this authority learning how to conquer their enemies. Very few trusted God. The only thing that kept them from being killed by God was their obedience to sacrifice a lamb every year at Passover (see Exodus 12) so God would "pass over" their sins. This lamb was a picture of God's promise to send that Messiah/Savior who would sacrifice His life on their behalf as did the sacrificial lambs. Eventually their stubborn self-dependence so got in the way that God could no longer be heard by them. This led to 400 years of absolute silence between them and God.

Jesus' Authority

Then Jesus, that promised Messiah (the word for Messiah in Greek is *Christ*) came and showed His creations how authority worked, as it should have been from the beginning. And at the end of His life, as planned, He redeemed them from the sin of forfeiting their God-given authority to Satan. This sacrificial *"Lamb of God, who takes away the sins of the world"* (John 1:29) came to create the way whereby the wrath of God would from now on pass over whoever would believe that His blood paid for their sins.

Sound familiar? Just as we can go to a pawn shop and buy back a treasure that a thief has stolen from us, so our Jesus, the Christ, paid for our sin of obeying God's enemy, that lying thief. Jesus exchanged His blood for our sin so that we can live with Him forever and not die when our body dies.

> *But now the righteousness of God without the law is manifested, being witnessed by the law and the prophets,*
> *Even the righteousness of God which is by faith of Jesus Christ unto all and upon all them that believe: for there is no difference.*

For all have sinned, and come short of the glory of God;

Being justified freely by his grace through the redemption that is in Christ Jesus,

Whom God hath set forth to be a propitiation through faith in his blood, to declare his righteousness for the remission of sins that are past, through the forbearance of God;

To declare, I say, at this time his righteousness: that he might be just, and the justifier of him which believeth in Jesus.

(Romans 3:21-26)

God could not come into a sin-sick, dirty soul. He had to clean it out first because He is holy and He hates sin. But once our sins are removed, we can ask Him to enter and be our Lord. Our new eternal life starts the minute we do this. All we have to do is believe that He did it for us, thank Him, and let Him *inside* of our once-again-cleaned soul. He comes into each of us individually when we invite Him. He gives each of us a fresh start. When we accept this, we are made innocent again like Adam and Eve, able to choose whom we will obey.

Our Authority

Paul knew this when he taught,

. . . his servants ye are whom ye obey.

(Romans 6:16)

Man had given the lordship of his life over to Satan by obeying him in the garden, and, from that point on, each man has had that choice as to whom he was going to obey. You may obey yourself, God, or Satan. When you obey yourself you're actually obeying Satan, the enemy of your soul. You hear and obey either God or Satan.

Paul explains it this way, that *"the creature [us] was made subject to vanity, not willingly but by reason of him who hath subjected the same in hope."* (Romans 8:20) God hoped each person would choose Him, even as He put within man this inclination to try to vainly do everything by himself by being self-dependent instead of God-dependent. How else would man have a choice to love God or not, if he had no temptation to live without God?

When your sins are removed, and you do not feel condemned by a God who has the right to kill you for your sinful self-centeredness, yet loved you enough to send His Son to die for your sins instead, you begin to *feel* like someone very special. You can put up your chin and say, "Yes, God, I am someone because *you* made me to be free of sin, and I am able to now learn authority over the things that come along in my life. It was *your* plan and promise, not mine. With You, I can have authority because now You are inside of me."

Jesus came to show us that authority which man had lost, and how to get it back again. *"Jesus taught as one having authority."* (Matthew 7:29, emphasis added) This is #1849 *exousia* = power.

Jesus *cast out demons* with authority. (Mark 1:27)

Jesus was given *"all authority."* (Matthew 28:18)

Jesus gave us all authority (Luke 9:1) *"All authority is given unto me . . . Go ye, therefore, in [My] name."* (Matthew 28:18-19). Remember in the Greek the word for name denotes the power, character, and authority of God the Father, God the Son, and God the Holy Spirit.

God's Plan of the Ages

Let's back off now and look at the whole picture.

From Adam to Abraham, *the first 2,000 years,* God mostly let His creations find out what it was like to live without the authority He had given Adam, which Adam had given away.

From Abraham to the first coming of Christ, *the second 2,000 years,* God taught His Israelites how to have authority over the Earth's nations.

From the first coming of Christ to the Second Coming of Christ, *the third 2,000 years,* He has been teaching those who have chosen Him how to have spiritual authority over Satan's kingdom of sin, sicknesses, and devils.

That's 6,000 years. The *seventh 1,000-year period will be the Millennium.* (No one is positive whenever that really starts. Our calendar years have been changed so much through ancient and modern history that we could be off at least three years one way or another.)

Welcome your generation's invitation, to enter the twenty-first century and its marvelous potential for your future as a predestined overcomer, *just as He said* throughout the Bible.

He said it to Adam in Genesis . . .have dominion.

He said it to the Israelites . . . go and conquer.

He said it to Jesus in the Gospels . . . all authority has been given back to Me, now you go in My name, and do the same.

He said it to us, through Paul in Romans. . . . predestined to be conformed into His likeness.

He said it to John in Revelation . . . you are to be overcomers.

He is saying it to us now . . . His plan has never changed.

He is saying it to you . . . NOW.

* * *

Chapter **3**

The Power of Agreement

"**D**on't go to those tent meetings!"

"Why?"

"Oh, that guy is a hoax. It's got to be trickery."

Tell that to the woman I saw lying on a stretcher, who got up and began walking at the insistence of a young, eager preacher. I was close enough to see her. She was visibly stronger and color returned to her face.

Praise God, she was really healed.

After that first eye-opening session I began to attend every night of the campaign. Since I was a pastor, I was invited to sit in the reserved section on the platform. I was elated to be able to view at close hand the healing evangelist, A. A. Allen, and found him to be a giant of faith. Even though he was maligned by the press, persecuted by his denomination, misunderstood by the churches, and hounded by the devil, Allen would tackle any disease and win. I thought to myself, "If he can do it, I can do it."

Soon after that I heard one of my friends say that he had seen Oral Roberts at a tent meeting in Phoenix. This well-known evangelist would command that people be well.

I remember thinking again, more strongly than ever, "Why not me?" God would work in *me!* So I tried it and it worked! My mind could somehow always remember and agree that the Word says, "*There is no respect* [favoritism, partiality] *of persons with God.*" (Romans 2:11) I figured that if God could use these men, God could use me.

There was no one less qualified to have authority to preach, heal the sick, and cast out demons than me. My soul was an emotional mess because of my upbringing. I was taught that I was a nobody. I have fought this all of my life.

But when I stepped out by faith and did what Jesus told His disciples to do, and used the power and authority as best as I knew how, then God did some wonderful healing through me.

As I studied more about God's Word, I learned a very important truth of spirit-soul-body agreement. This principle helps to explain how salvation, physical healing, and emotional healing work. It also helps us understand our role in ministering healing and deliverance to others.

If I would use my mouth to command that the sick be made well, God would keep His part of the bargain and they would be well.

I did not know back then, that when my spirit and my mouth were in agreement, my emotional soul would submit to the other two. But now I can see that that "two-against-one" principle was at work, so that all three were coming into agreement. And if a "nobody" like me can, you can. We were *all* called to be Overcomers with authority, not just some of us. And whether the problems are in you, or in somebody else, God still can use *you* to overcome them.

How Does Agreement Work?

Overcomers are interesting folks. They are a spirit, they have a soul, and they live inside a body. Say that again:

I AM a spirit . . . it is who I am.

I HAVE a soul . . . it is my chooser.

and *I LIVE INSIDE* a body . . . it is just my casing.

These God-built creations have within them the most awesome predestined potential to have authority when they can each get their spirit, soul, and body to agree.

Overcomers can learn to keep their spirits in charge over their souls and their bodies. Our spirit is stronger than our flesh, but only if we choose to obey our spirit with our souls.

Father, Son, and Holy Spirit Agree

Interestingly, we are a three-part being just like God is Triune. Paul says in 1 Thessalonians 5:23, *"I pray God your whole spirit and soul and body be preserved blameless unto the coming of our Lord Jesus Christ."*

The whole Bible is full of this three-ness. In the beginning God created *us* by saying , *"Let* us *make man in* our *image, after* our *likeness."* (Genesis 1:26, emphasis added) Who was He (God, the Father) talking to? Jesus said that He, Himself, had been there when the Earth was being made. *"Glorify thou me with . . . the glory which I had with thee before the world was."* (John 17:5) So the Father was talking to Jesus about this new human being they were about to create. And the third part of this Trinity-God, the Holy Spirit, was there hovering over the whole thing. *"And the Spirit of God moved upon the face of the waters."* (Genesis 1:2).

God the Father, God the Son, and God the Holy Spirit making man in their "image and likeness:" one Godhead in three Persons creating man with three parts—spirit, soul, and body. (1 John 5:7) Adam was to overcome anything with his God-breathed, three-sided nature.

It is only when we can get these three in us to agree that we can keep that authority working and remain overcomers in today's world.

The Body

Think of the stories you've heard about people who have been mortally wounded, who died and were able to leave their bodies and look down at some doctor or nurse bending over them in an emergency hospital room trying to bring them back to life, or pulling a sheet over their head. This is their spirit looking down on their body.

So we have a body, an "earth-suit." That's obvious. Our spirit, given the right circumstances, can leave our body and look back at our death.

The Soul

What's the soul? Genesis 2:7 says, *"And the LORD God formed man of the dust of the ground, and breathed into his nostrils the breath of life: and man became a living soul,"* (*ne-phesh* in the Hebrew, "a breathed-on being"). The soul is the will, mind, and emotions. We have these and so do the animals. (More later on how the soul works.)

The animals (created just ahead of man) were called "creatures" which also means "souls," so they have wills, minds, and emotions like us.

The Spirit

Man alone got an added thing . . . some of God's breath – *ruah* = spirit. Because of this added spirit, man became a *living* soul; one that would *live forever*. This is a huge step up from animals, who have bodies and souls, but *not* spirits. Spirits, that is you and I, (remember you *are* a spirit), have insights, imaginations, creative abilities, and a communication with God that the animals do not. This part of us, the spirit, is the place into which God comes to abide with us when we have asked Jesus to wash us clean with His blood, and ask Him to re-ignite us by inviting Him to come inside us to rule us from within. It is here in our spirits where we are born again as Jesus commanded in John 3:7. This is where He makes us perfect.

The Struggle to Be Perfect

People think you mean perfect in your soul, whereas perfect in the Greek means complete. Your spirit is made perfect.

You have met people who do everything right in every possible way and feel that having done that makes them "spiritual" Christians. What they don't realize is that everything they're doing is *soulish*. We are, in effect, trying too hard to do it. We're doing it in our own strength, our own ability, and possibly for our own motives.

Ever wonder why He said we have to be "perfect" and you *knew* you were *not* perfect when you read it? *"Be ye, therefore, perfect even as your Father . . . is perfect."* (Matthew 5:48) Sure! Perfect? Me? No way. Yes, your spirit is made perfect by His cleansing blood. It is your soul that is not perfect. But He is your righteousness because you let Him wash your sins away and *He* made your human spirit perfect. *"Christ* in *you,* [is the] *hope of glory . . . that we may present every man* perfect *in Christ Jesus."* (Colossians 1:27,28, emphasis added)

Only individual humans have the ability to ask God, to welcome Him, inside their human spirits, rebirthing their spirits by His invited presence. He gave us the *"gift of righteousness"* (Romans 5:17) so that we would no longer be afraid of Him. When things are all right between you and God in your spirit, then your soul can hear that from your nearby spirit, and keep guilt from interfering while God is speaking to your soul.

You had an imperfect spirit before you were born again. Once your spirit became perfect in Christ, it becomes your soul that needs daily renewing. It is our will, mind and emotions that need to be retrained and convinced that Jesus reinstated our right to have *Authority.* He said, *"All power"* (exousia, #1849 = authority, right, jurisdiction) *"is given unto me. . . . Go ye, therefore, and teach all nations, baptizing them in the name of the Father, and of the Son, and of the Holy Ghost.* " (Matthew 28:18)

Name means "onoma," the character of each of the persons in the Godhead. It is this seed-part-spirit of us into which He comes to empower us. This is how we gain authority to rule the world.

The Soul Is the Chooser

Our souls are choosers. Our souls can either choose to obey God in our born-again spirits or obey our spoiled, self-centered bodies where sin lies. We have to keep remembering that our soul is a reactor, a storer and deducer of many thoughts. It reacts, digests, thinks, arranges the worldly input and tries to make sense of it. Here is where overcoming takes place next, after your spirit is born again. Here is where you seek daily to *"be not conformed to this world, but be ye transformed by the renewing of your mind* (part of your soul), *that ye may prove what is that good, and acceptable, and perfect, will of God."* (Romans 12:2).

It is your soul that needs to agree with your spirit which already knows what is right. Your spirit instinctively knows the Word of God and your soul would like to, but it has to be trained to agree with God and the real you in your spirit.

My mind has acquired a great deal of junk that I have put into it since the day I was born. There are a lot of words in there to fight off and to replace with His words and His thoughts. There is a great amount of old worldly stuff in my soul that is influencing my behavior and feelings that just aren't true. I have "reasonable" opinions, assumptions, and deductions which I'm not sure are true. They are both conscious and unconscious. It is this *soulish* junk which needs to be removed, and replaced by the new, clean truth that Jesus returns to us.

"I am the way, the truth, and the life; no man cometh unto the Father, but by Me." (John 14:6). The teaching used by so many that no one comes to the Father except the Spirit draws him is totally false. The Spirit does not draw, he convicts. Pastors quote this incorrectly over and over. The Father draws to Jesus, and Jesus draws us to the Father.

In the beginning was the Word, and the Word was with God, and the Word was God.
(John 1:1)

That's why we need to read the truth, God's Word, *His* words, everyday. Everyday the world system we live in keeps slamming new words into our souls that aren't true. So we must keep planting fresh truth in there to combat both the old beliefs and the new errors of thinking we accumulate. Wishy-washy feelings are calmed only by His solid truth.

The Word of God helps me to decipher the difference between what my soul is feeling and what my spirit knows is the truth.

The word of God is quick, and powerful, and sharper than any two-edged sword, piercing even to the dividing asunder [apart] *of soul and*

spirit, and of the joints and marrow, and is a discerner of the thoughts and intents of the heart.
(Hebrews 4:12)

No wonder I can talk with myself. My soul and spirit are separate and talk to each other.

The Example of King David

David knew this when his spirit told his soul, *"Bless the LORD, O my soul, and forget not all his benefits."* (Psalm 103:1) Who was talking? David's spirit. Who was listening? His soul. His will, mind, and emotions (his soul) were in a mess, and he was telling them to line up with what his spirit knew was true about God's provision for him. So he told his soul to praise God instead of worrying. He was commanding his soul to line up with what his spirit knew was true. His soul could choose not to if it wished, and he could have stayed in the dumps of depression if he felt like it. But he chose to and began to praise the Lord instead. His spirit and his soul came into agreement.

In essence, he said, "Hey soul, this is David speaking to you. You just calm down in there and obey me, because God has said He would take care of us and he's going to. So just knock it off, and settle down and bless the Lord, O, my soul!" That's how he got emotional and mental wholeness and victory. We can do it the same way, and end up having the same victories he experienced.

Can Satan Read Our Minds?

We do not have any original thoughts, just deducted ones. They are all spirit, either godly or evil. Jesus told us that His words (or His thoughts spoken out loud, if you will) were spirit. *"The words that I speak unto you, they are spirit, and they are life."* (John 6:63)

People say, *"Can Satan read your thoughts?"* No, the demons all around you just read your actions and predict from them what you are apt to do. Then they send "fiery darts" (i.e., thoughts) to your brain, hoping to make you think they're your own, tempting you according to what they see in your countenance and your moods from the outside. Paul told us about those in Ephesians 6:16, *"Above all, taking the shield of faith, with which ye shall be able to quench all the fiery darts of the wicked."* It's just the way the people around you can "read you." They can almost predict what you're going to do, or what you're thinking, by your behavior, by the look on your face, and by what you say. The demons do that too, and throw thoughts at you accordingly. You think they're your thoughts because you hear them in your head. They're being sent, but you don't have to receive them.

Unless you're wise to them, you will think, "My, what an awful person I am to think that thought! " Or, "Sure, I'll do that!"

How to Get Rid of Bad Thoughts

We should be deciphering which thoughts are God's and match His written Word, and which thoughts are from the enemy. If they don't match the Word of God, they are not of God, and the real you (spirit) can confidently respond by saying, out loud, "Oh no, you don't . . . that's not me! That's you, dummy. Be gone!"

Don't just try to stop thinking bad thoughts, tell them out loud to go away. When your spirit (the real you), your soul (your will, mind, and emotions) and your body (your mouth) have agreed in this way, a three-way agreement, you will have used the three-sided overcoming power Jesus gave you.

God wanted us to be set free, with His authority in us, from the corruptions of this world. Check out the next part of that verse we looked at about how God set it up.

For the creature was made subject to vanity, not willingly but by reason of him who hath subjected the same in hope, Because the creature itself also shall be delivered from the bondage of corruption into the glorious liberty of the children of God. (Romans 8:20-21)

Liberty. Freedom. Jesus was free. We can be, too.

The Example of Jesus

How did Jesus stay in charge? What did He know that seems to elude us? Most importantly, He was in total agreement with His Father.

As He stood there before the dead Lazarus, He knew that if He determined in His *soul* to speak with His mouth (His *body*) the words which He heard from His Father in His *spirit*, that the dead had to rise. If His spirit, soul, and body were in agreement, He had authority over anything.

Anything? Yes, because this was true and He believed it, He could do it. Because He knew this worked, the sicknesses, diseases, demons, and death were within His control. We must know it and believe it in the very same way. You have whatsoever you believe (Mark 11:23,24) and when you believe what He believed, you become an imitator of Christ (1 Corinthians 4:16), an overcomer, more and more like Him every day. When you know this truth, the truth will set you *free.* (John 8:32)

How Can I Do This?

To be in charge of every situation where the Holy Spirit is leading you requires the cooperation of your spirit in which God dwells, what your soul determines to believe, and the movement of your body. Get any two to agree and the third will come into line. Two against one . . . and the third will agree. Who's in charge? The spirit, over the soul, over the body. All three. Then nothing can stand in an overcomer's way.

Let's look at this principle of getting two of the three parts of yourself to agree in order to get the third to line up. This will work in all three directions. Words develop your character. This is why Jesus said, *"The words that I speak unto you, they are spirit and they are life"* (John 6:63) *and "Now ye are clean through the word which I have spoken unto you."* (John 15:3)

For instance:

If you get your words (body) and your soul (will, mind and emotions) to line up with the words of God that Jesus is Lord, your spirit is saved.

That is why when you decided to say that Jesus is Lord, He comes into your spirit and it is born again. When you decide (soul) to say out loud (body), "Yes," your spirit gets changed into a born-again one. *"If thou shalt confess with thy mouth* [body] *the Lord Jesus, and shalt believe in thine heart* [soul] *that God hath raised him from the dead, thou shalt be saved* [spirit]. *"* (Romans 10:9)

Body's Words + Soul = Change in Your Spirit

If you get your mouth (body) to say the words that your spirit is now filled with (the Word), your soul (feelings and emotions) will fall in line. That is why David would say, "Bless the LORD, O my soul," so that he could feel his emotions of fear and anxiety settling down in his soul. This is how depression, anxiety, and many mental illnesses and dysfunctional behaviors are changed. We encourage our people to get their real born-again selves (spirit) to tell their emotions (soul) *out loud* (body) that God's Word is true on whatever issue they are dealing with, then their emotions settle down. This is the renewing of your mind (see Romans 12:2).

Body's Words + Spirit = Change in Your Soul

If you fill your mind (soul) with the words that match your Word-filled spirit, *then* your words (body) will change. You can speak to your body and it will line up and be healed. *"Out of the abundance of the heart the mouth speaketh."* (Matthew 12:34) So stay in the Word every day until you believe it and your mouth agrees.

Spirit's Words + Soul = Change in Your Body

Your three-part self can be used of God to bring healing and deliverance to others. Your perfection in your spirit, your renewing of your soul, and your healing of your body will make you an overcomer. Then you can confidently minister to others.

There are days when my own body will not obey my words, but when I get my words (mouth) to agree with my spirit and my soul, others are healed. I command their bodies to agree with my spirit and my soul, and they are healed. When my spirit and my soul agree with my mouth that God's will is for us to be healed, then they are healed.

What About Soul-power?

The Holy Spirit used Watchman Nee to teach me about soul-power. When I first read his book, *The Latent Power of the Soul,* I did not like it. I thought to myself, "Boy, were you off base on this, Watchman!" Then, a few years later I watched three men who had leadership power over people, and God showed me that they were operating in a very real power that was not of God. They could get people to obey them.

Soul-power was removed from Adam when he fell, but there are people who have learned how to use it and it can be dangerous to those with whom they are dealing.

To use soul-power is to develop the strength of mind-will-emotions to establish yourself to have power over others. Jesus wants us to have His power in our spirits.

Jesus, the Center of the reason for the existence of this Universe, is looking to find those whose desire is to be made into His likeness *for* Him. He wants the victory to be ours so that we can be *His.*

Your authority is no stronger than the King who sits on the throne of your life. We have a tendency to get carried away with authority so we sometimes forget to check and make sure that Christ is the reason we are overcoming. Jesus warned his disciples about the same thing.

Behold, I give unto you power to tread on
serpents and scorpions,
    and over all the power of the enemy:
    and nothing shall by any means hurt you.
    Notwithstanding, in this rejoice not, that the
spirits are subject unto you;
    but rather rejoice, because your names are
written in heaven. (Luke 10:19,20)

If you catch yourself slipping and getting back on the throne (i.e., overcoming because it feels so good to be in charge over others), then stop and repent. Get the wrong king off the throne. Consciously tell Jesus again that He has the right to be center stage, and not you. You do not want to reign with soul-power. Your spirit cannot rule and reign over your soul and body if the child of the king is sitting where the King belongs.

When you repent, you will sense the cleansing that opens up your now-humbled spirit. You can then regain the corrected authority to command the demons or sicknesses to obey you.

Avoid Being "Double-minded"

It's possible to approach a church service with the desire and anticipation to worship God, but then get into the flesh or soulish realm. This makes us "double-minded" and we can expect that God will not hear us.

For let not that man think that he shall receive
anything of the Lord.
    A double-minded man is unstable in all his ways.
                (James 1:7,8)

Gilda, a young woman who attends a church in this area, is a good example. She throws herself into the music. During the worship service she gyrates, jerks, points, and moves around to such an extent that it's annoying to people even several rows away. Perhaps she may have begun to worship God in her spirit, but now her flesh has taken over. She is allowing her emotions to drive her body, possibly even doing things for effect.

We must examine our behavior, our practices, our traditions to see if there are contradictions between what we believe and what we do. We must check ourselves out against the Word of God to see if we line up with the truth.

Our goal should be to get the agreement of our spirits, souls, and bodies to agree with HIM.

* * *

Chapter **4**

Man-made Hindrances to Our Authority

I stood nervously before the TV cameras and tried to put into words a lifetime of 45 years of serving God. Given only 25 minutes, I was silently praying and trusting. But to my dismay one of my points was terribly misunderstood by several influential people. Their phone calls to the station manager led her to cancel any further TV interviews or appearances on the Christian channel.

I tried to teach the churches too much, too soon, too fast. Try to avoid this type of confusion.

This type of confusion will rob you of the authority God wants you to have: authority to heal, to deliver those in bondage, and to live a God-honoring life.

It may mean rethinking some long-held traditions and practices in your church or denomination. It may mean having a long talk with God. It may mean taking a new stand for Bible truth. Are you willing to be open-minded? Are you willing for the Holy Spirit to teach you, even if that means to correct you?

Who Is Obeying God?

Why aren't believers doing the "greater things" that Jesus said we would do? How many people do you know personally who are living in day-to-day victory? How many people do you know who are healing others? How many people do you know who are performing deliverances? Jesus said it clearly. We have the fivefold commission, the Great Commission, and the Holy Spirit's indwelling power. What's going on?

We have *substituted* man-made ideas and understandings in place of the authority that He gave us. We have depended on religious procedures and catchy clichés, instead of developing the character and authority of Christ *in* us.

Five Main Problems

I have identified five main problems here. Ask the Holy Spirit to reveal the truth to you as you read this chapter. Be open to correction that He points out.

1. Plead the Blood

The blood! What a powerful gift of God, the only thing strong enough to cover our sins and make us right with God. The only thing that can keep us from the wrath of God. The only thing that will get us into heaven. Nothing in the world or in heaven above can take its place or do what it does. That most precious blood covenant is God's perfect will and plan for all of us. We cannot hear from God if sin comes between us and Him. We cannot get rid of those sins unless we accept the blood of Christ as our gift from God.

But a misuse of the blood has crept into the Church. It is called "pleading the blood." Look it up in an exhaustive Bible concordance. You will not find this phrase anywhere.

We must be careful not to fall into the new cliché traps of each generation or denomination of the past. "Pleading the blood" has become one such cliché of this generation, and this phrase, *used wrongly*, is powerless in healing and demonic warfare because it is not scriptural. If it were right, Jesus would have used it.

In fact, every mention of the word "plead" in all its forms is mentioned only in the Old Testament. It means "to beg for." Of course back then, before the blood was freely given by Christ, mercy had to be begged for. But then Christ *gave* us His blood freely. We never have to beg for it now. We ask for forgiveness and thank Him that He already provided the blood that takes away every sin. It's done. We can remind God how wonderful He is to have provided that wonderful way to be free of our sins, but we don't beg for it.

Those who use this phrase are generally referring to the truth that once you have been born again by receiving forgiveness through the blood of Jesus, then legally He is our Lord and nothing can separate us from God from then on. That is absolutely right. The great conclusion of Paul's marvelous discourse in Romans 8:31-39 *says,* Nothing can *"separate us from the love of God, which is in Christ Jesus, our Lord."* (verse 39) I count on that all the time!

But believers use that phrase, "plead the blood" as though the blood was there to protect us from Satan and his demonic forces. That is not true. It does not. It protects us from the wrath of God. Romans 5, verses 8 and 9, says, *"God commendeth his love toward us in that, while we were yet sinners, Christ died for us. Much more then, being now justified by his blood, we shall be saved from wrath though him."*

In Exodus, it was the blood of the lamb on the doorposts of the first Passover that protected the Israelites from the promise that *God* would kill the firstborn male of every family, unless the blood had been placed there. *"For the LORD will pass through to smite the Egyptians; and when he seeth the blood upon the lintel, and on the two side posts, the LORD will pass over the door, and will not allow the destroyer to come into your houses to smite you."* (Exodus 12:23, emphasis added) In each case, it was God's decision—not Satan's—whether or not to use the destroyer to kill. It was God and His wrath masterminding each individual death.

He says it again in Exodus 12:29: *"And it came to pass . . . the* LORD *smote all the firstborn in the land of Egypt."* (emphasis added) The blood didn't keep the people from Satan's intent; it kept them from God's intent. *The blood saves us from the wrath of God.*

And so it is that Christ's blood cleanses out our spirit thoroughly when we are born again, allowing Him entrance into a newly sinless place. The blood then daily cleanses our soul as we ask forgiveness while walking in our new lives in Christ.

The blood of Christ does not clean out the body from the sicknesses or demons that have been in it before we became Christians or have entered into it since then. Only commanding them to leave, with Christ's authority, makes them leave.

You cannot "cover yourself with the blood" and expect everyday happenings to keep you from getting sick. We still get sick in *our physical bodies,* and demons can still enter into *our physical bodies.* It is dramatic trauma, or consistent intentional sinning, that opens doors to demons, allowing them to enter our bodies.

The blood neither keeps demons from coming into our bodies or homes nor removes them. Only using our authority in Christ, and His covenant with us, can do that.

When you got saved, your wrinkles and sicknesses and/or demons did not go away. Your spirit was reborn, but your body was not. Paul knew that sins were in his *body* after he was saved. (Romans 7:18) *"For I know that in me (that is in my flesh) dwelleth no good thing."*

If we "plead the blood," *instead* of commanding sicknesses and demons to leave (exactly as Jesus did and commanded us to do in Matthew 10:8 and 28:20), we will continue to be less effective in healing and deliverance than He intended us to be. Reading, Ephesians 6:11-16, tells us to use the *Word* against demonic forces. He does not say to "use" the blood.

It is that wonderful inside *knowing* that the blood has made us right with God which gives us the confidence to command sin, sicknesses, and demons to be removed. The blood makes us righteous with God. It restores our relationship with Him, making it like the relationship Jesus had with God, so that sin does not block our ability to hear Him.

The reason Jesus could have authority over diseases and demons was that He could hear what to do because His soul (will, mind, and emotions) was uncluttered with sin and His mind was set on the will of the Father. But that did not keep the devil away from Him in the garden. It was only His audible command that Satan leave Him that made Satan depart.

Peter and Paul both teach about the blood, but they never "used" it or said "I plead the blood" when they healed or cast out demons, as we have erroneously learned to do from religious doctrines. Let us follow Jesus' examples only. Then we will have less failures as we obey God to *heal the sick and cast out demons.* (Matthew 10:8; 28:20; Mark 16:18)

2. Christians Cannot Have Demons

Many people insist that the presence of Jesus and His Holy Spirit within a Christian automatically repels all demonic forces. We have found this not to be true. Consider this.

We have had in our deliverance ministry of almost 40 years, hundreds of good Christians come to us with some horrible problem that they could not gain control of, despite their victories in Christ in many other areas of their lives. These are often born-again, church-going believers who have gone for the best counseling, read the Word daily, had weekly fellowship with the Body of Christ, and were still plagued. What was the problem?

The problem was that they did not understand that demons lodge *in the body, not in the spirit or the soul* (unless a person has deliberately given his life to the devil by some evil covenant), just as sicknesses still remain, or get into, the body of one who is a true believer.

We are the picture of the Old Testament Temple. First Corinthians 3:16 tells us that we are the temple of the Holy Spirit. The temple had three parts, just as we have three parts: spirit, soul, and body. Our spirits are like the Holy of Holies where God lived in the Ark. Our souls are like the inner court where the services were conducted and the Word of God was heard. The outer court was where all sorts of *both* good and evil things went on. Likewise, demons in Christians are in their bodies, not in their thirsting souls or born-again spirits.

Think: did God's mighty presence in the Throne Room of heaven keep Satan from coming to visit there in Job's time? (Job 1:6) No. In fact, God was having a conversation with him. Then again, in Ahab's time, a lying evil spirit was given permission by God in Heaven to go and be a lying spirit to persuade Ahab. (1 Kings 22:22) Did the magnificent presence of Jesus in the wilderness temptation keep Satan away? *No!* (Matthew 4)

In each of these experiences neither Satan nor the devils ever left until commanded, out loud, to do so. In the same way, the presence of God in our spirits does not dispel the presence of demons in our bodies *until* someone commands them, out loud, to leave.

In deliverance from evil spirits, those with Christ's authority must audibly command the demons *to leave the body of the person*, just as Jesus did, and only as Jesus did. In obedience, I have learned to do this for over 40 years. You can do the same.

Trauma. Either emotional or physical trauma are entrances for evil spirits into *our bodies*. We can practically *always* trace the demons which had come into people who are delivered back to a time where an accident (especially head injuries), a crisis, drugs, immense sinning, or some other trauma had occurred, a time they can remember they were out of control.

Cleansed, born-again Christians must learn how to command demons to get out, and stay out, of their *bodies*.

If you are a Christian but something is out of your control and just won't let go, consider that demons may be the problem.

3. Saying "the Name of Jesus" Will Heal Diseases and Make Demons Flee

How many times have you heard the phrase, "in the name of Jesus" repeated over and over again as if it were some magical cure-all charm? I believe we use it too often without knowing what it means. I have heard pastors preach that just using the phrase "in the name of Jesus" gives us authority and the devils flee when they hear it. We have learned that this is not so.

I thoroughly believe in the name of Jesus. This is because, as I said earlier, the word *name* means *character and authority*. (Greek = *onoma* #3683 [all numbers given correspond to those in *Strong's Exhaustive Concordance*). It does not mean to use the word *Jesus* itself. It means we have acquired the character and authority of Jesus. It means to contain the personality of Jesus—His emotions, His beliefs, His attitudes, His motives, Him. We get this by a daily, intimate relationship with Him, and letting the Holy Spirit, whom He sent to us, renew our minds to become like His as we read and meditate on His Word.

This comes from our obedience to abide in Him and let Him abide in us. *"Abide in me, and I in you."* (John 15:4) This changes our old soulish natures into His powerful one. This changes our old beliefs into His beliefs, and *then* we get what we believe. *"Whatsoever things ye desire, when ye pray, believe that ye receive them, and [then] ye shall have them"* (Mark 11:24) His character and authority are in you, but it won't work unless you believe it. When you know that you know this, when you let yourself be convinced that His Word is true, *then* you will come in His name, the "name of Jesus," and be used of God to do the works of God. You won't have to use some cliché to boost your faith.

How much time do you spend daily in His presence in prayer, in His Word, and in His service, becoming like Him by close association with Him? How often do you ask the Holy Spirit to show you Jesus, and how to be like Him?

Don't just say His name, but come to every situation with your old character replaced by His character and authority. Our minds must be renewed to the point where we automatically think and react like He did. This takes time. Once we have invited Jesus to be our Savior and Lord, He then takes up residence inside our bodies within our spirit.

This new character and authority are "His name." This is coming to every circumstance and ministry *in the name of Jesus*. We can't just say His name and expect the sicknesses and demons to obey. It never says to *"say"* the name of Jesus." Jesus said,

"I am come in my Father's name," (John 5:43), but never once did He ever say, "Be healed in the name of my Father."

He had the character and the authority of His Father. We also must come in His *character and authority.* But first we must know that we know, within the depths of our being down to the tips of our fingers and toes, that His character and authority, developed in us, does the work. We *teach* this first, so that He gets the glory, just like Jesus who taught that, *"The Father that dwells in me, He does the works"* (John 14:10) But Jesus didn't say "I heal you in the name of the Father" even once *during* healing or deliverance. He must be our example.

The Name of Jesus Is Something We Are to *Be*, Not Something We Are to *Say*

This is not to say that I never say the name of Jesus. I say it every day in one way or another. That word should be part of our normal everyday conversation. Our children and our churches should be hearing and saying that name easily, as easily as we say our spouse's names or our children's names. Jesus is the most important person in our life and His name should be on our lips constantly as a natural consequence of our daily dependence on Him.

A few years ago my wife, Marilee, hit her head on the windshield of my truck when she and I were in an accident. When I saw her hair hanging from the windshield, which she had just hit hard and bounced off of, and saw the blood on her forehead, all this mighty man of God could do was lay my hand on her forehead and say, "Jesus, Jesus, Jesus!" But I *knew* what I meant! She was totally healed and suffered no consequences as expected. The ambulance attendants, the emergency x-ray technicians, and the hospital doctor gave us dire warnings about what could be internally wrong in her head (although they could find nothing in the x-rays).

But I did not start saying "Jesus, Jesus, Jesus" from then on as a way to get people healed. It was His presence and the authority of the character of Jesus which the Holy Spirit had developed in me that brought about that healing. It was because I expected her to be healed, as Jesus would also have at the touch of His hand.

This was only one in hundreds of other healings where I have been used of God, where I did not intentionally *say* His name but rather *believed* in His name. And in many of those other healings I said the name of Jesus, not to "get the job done," but just as a normal consequence of conversation.

We must keep watching for what *Jesus* did, and do it instead of relying on worn-out teachings and phrases.

How many times will we say we act like Jesus, and then go on doing what we have heard and seen others do, without researching for ourselves what the Word says?

How much longer are we going to imitate the mistakes of the past instead of doing our own homework, searching the Scriptures to learn how Jesus did it?

4. Anointing With Oil Will Heal Them

This one is touchy to many people, so please read all of it before drawing your conclusions. Ask the Holy Spirit to reveal the truth to you.

It always made me uncomfortable to see people use oil. I wondered why the Holy Spirit never impressed on me to use oil in healing or deliverance. I didn't want to be left out of something, and I sure hated to be *not* doing something since it made me stand out like a sore thumb when others were doing it so freely. But I never saw that Jesus *ever* used oil, even once.

I find a great many references to oil in the Old Testament, all referring to cooking, the preparations of sacrificial offerings, lamp oil, anointing men and/or temple articles for God's service, or as medicine directly applied on a wound. None of it was used as anointing for healing.

There are a few references to oil in the New Testament. Let's look at them all.

Matthew 25:3-8—the story of the ten virgins who took oil for their lamps. This has nothing to do with healing.

Luke 7:46—Jesus rebuked his host for not anointing His head with oil.

Luke 10:34—the story of the Samaritan pouring oil and wine directly into the wounds of the man who had been beaten on the road.

Luke 16:6—refers to the hundred measures of oil on the steward's bill.

Hebrew 1:19—refers metaphorically to the "oil of gladness."

Revelation 6:6— "hurt not the oil and the wine" is end-time symbolism.

Revelation 18:13—refers to many of the traded goods in mercantilism.

None of these verses I've noted refer to oil used for healing. There are two verses remaining. Let's look at them carefully in their context.

Mark 6:13 is one notable exception, where it says that the twelve disciples *"cast out many devils, and anointed with oil many that were sick, and healed them. "* (emphasis added) This, in the light of the fact that Jesus had just told them to *"take nothing for their journey, save a staff only; no scrip, no bread, no money in their purse. "* (verse 8, emphasis added) He did not mention oil, nor commend them for doing it that way. This was an addition of theirs, and He did not admonish them for doing it because they were young in their faith and had much to learn. Also, there is an *"and"* between their placing *"oil* [on] *many that were sick"* and the words *"healed them, "* indicating that the oil had nothing to do with the supernatural healing that came. Most important here is the fact that He *never* taught them to do it.

If the oil was so important and it accomplished the healing, we should then be worried about what *kind* of oil to use. Would thicker oil be more effective than thin? Would crankcase oil be better than vegetable oil? Would baby oil be better than canola? See how depending on oil can get us out of touch with the reality of who we are in Him? We would depend on "stuff" instead of what He has made us to be for His glory.

This is the reason Jesus told His disciples to take *nothing,* so that every situation would *demand* of them that they use their faith and nothing else. This is how their faith increased by use. Whatever they *used* would be what gained strength. This is why they came home exclaiming that they had been successful.

Recently I saw again how this principle applied to my ministry. Ruth used to live in Arizona before she moved to Oregon with her two sons. They were used to being healed here where I could "get my hands on them." Now they call, place their hands on whatever afflicted area where they need healing, and I command that illness to be gone. And it goes, every time.

I realized the other day that she and her sons absolutely demand of me that I heal them. That *demand* draws the faith out of me. There is no oil or physical contact to rely on, so I *have to* rely on the character and authority of Christ Jesus which the Holy Spirit has wrought in me, and *that* is what brings about their healing so effectively.

The second verse is **James 5:14**, ". . . anointing him with oil in the name of the Lord Jesus." This is the only verse believers can turn to when they try to justify anointing the sick with oil. First of all, remember that this is the *only* place in the Word where it is mentioned in this fashion. I always look for three verses in order to justify how I minister. (For instance, I lay hands on the sick because it is mentioned many times.)

But look at the context of this letter of exhortation from Paul. In this case, they had lost their sense of anointing by sinning in the ways Paul had just been extensively reprimanding them for, and exhorting them about, in the previous paragraphs of his letter. They needed the oil in this one instance to remind them of the very serious responsibility of the authority they had been given as elders to walk in the character and authority of Christ. Anointing with oil had been used previously when they had been appointed to become used of God for His service. Here it was used to help them *regain* that originally ordained sense of authority over the sickness of those to whom they were ministering so healing could come in the name of Jesus.

Therefore, we should not take this verse and make a whole new doctrine of using oil, as if it were the oil that brought about the healing. We should have had oil used on us when we were ordained to show us and others that we have been selected to be used for His holy calling. This matches the many Old Testament scriptures of anointing men for service. To use it in healing is to demand that the oil do something that we should be demanding of ourselves and our faith in the God who ministers through us in His character and authority.

5. Paul's Thorn in the Flesh and Job's Sufferings

People who want to avoid dealing with the issue of sickness and healing often fall back on the "thorn in the flesh" that Paul had or the problem of Job's suffering. Neither one of these examples proves that sickness is something we have to just live with and not overcome. Let's look at these verses more carefully. Paul said,

> *And lest I should be exalted above measure through the abundance of the revelations, there was given to me a thorn in the flesh, the messenger of Satan to buffet me, lest I should be exalted above measure. (2 Corinthians 12:7)*

Notice that Paul goes on to clarify that the thorn was a messenger from Satan. A messenger is a person, not a sickness. Being a master of Old Testament scripture Paul was using the word "thorn" the way it was used in the following verses.

> *Know for a certainty that the LORD your God will no more drive out any of these nations from before you; but they shall be snares and traps unto you, and scourges in your sides, and thorns in your eyes, until ye perish from off this good land which the LORD your God hath given you.* (Joshua 23:13)

Wherefore I also said, I will not drive them out from before you, but they shall be as thorns in your sides, and their gods shall be a snare unto you. (Judges 2:3)

Can you see how the word "thorn" refers to people? Paul certainly was buffeted by various people who came against him. Look back to verse 30 of 2 Corinthians 11 and read the entire chapter where he lists his infirmities. None of them are illnesses at all; they were persecutions. After writing this to the church at Corinth he went on, strong and healthy, as we read in Acts 16, 17, and 18. The reason we know this is because in the next chapter it says that he was in Philippi, headed to Corinth for the third time. (2 Corinthians 13:1,14)

And what about 2 Corinthians 12:8 where Paul asked God three times to take "the thorn in the flesh" away? If you read this in context, it's clearly the false prophets and harassing persons (2 Corinthians 11:13).

Many people worry about Job. He seemed to be so perfect. It almost strikes fear in our hearts that if we attain to a higher level of goodness in our life, God will unleash Satan upon us to make us "sick, for the glory of God."

Satan didn't make Job sick. Job's fear caused his problem. "For the thing which I greatly feared is come upon me, and that which I was afraid of is come unto me." (Job 3:25) It was made worse by his self-righteousness. After he repented (Job 42:6,10), he was healed, the Lord gave him twice as much, and he lived to see his sons' sons to the fourth generation.

The trouble he had only lasted for a few months out of his 140 years of life. (Job 42:16) God's intent had been to make him stronger, not keep him sick.

We Must Learn the Truth

So watch out for those deceiving clichés, dear Christian. If your denominational doctrines, your pastor's preaching, or your Bible study class doesn't match up with the Word of God that you have gained from your own personal daily renewing of your mind in Scriptures, then don't keep on reliving their mistakes. You have an obligation to go to them and ask, "Why?" They, too, must hear it fresh from obedient sheep. Leaders must be challenged by learners, as long as we have the Word written for our continuous rethinking.

All scripture is given by inspiration of God, and is profitable for doctrine, for reproof, for correction, *for instruction in righteousness.*
(2 Timothy 3:16, emphasis added)

"For correction" shows us our responsibility to be *both* correctable *and* to correct our brothers and sisters in love.

We don't need arrogance to be obedient to God. But we *do* need to be obedient as we refer one another to the Word and correct and exhort one another in love.

But the wisdom that is from above is first pure, then peaceable, gentle, and easy to be entreated, *full of mercy and good fruits, without partiality, and without hypocrisy. And the fruit of righteousness is sown in peace of them that make peace.* (James 3:17,18, emphasis added) (#2138 entreated = "easily persuaded" by the truth, "compliant.") Are you easily entreated?

Let's weed out *all* the religious clichés we can find. Ask the Holy Spirit to show you anything you have let sneak into your understanding which is blocking the very best ministry God is calling you to. The body of Christ needs maturing in this area in these last days because we are going to be called on to be the best soldiers the world has ever known. *Then* the end will come, and He can call His wife "Perfect!" In the meantime His Bride must be determine to be "perfected" by the Word and His Holy Spirit. ✝

* * *

Chapter **5**

The Truth About Satan and Evil Spirits

The truth that there are evil spirits is straight from the Bible. Jesus cast them out of people, even healed people. Why should we think there are no more evil spirits? It was not a psychological problem then and it is not merely psychological now. There are actual demonic spirits and they torment people.

People are now more willing to hear about angels and demons. Along with the current fascination with angels has come a new acceptance and belief in the fallen spirits, heightened by an attraction to the occult. Some churches have begun to take a more in-depth interest in order to get family members out of cults. The police, especially ones in the inner cities, are being trained in finding and exposing satanic violent crimes. If you're too sophisticated to believe in demons, just ask the teenagers in your neighborhood about the weird things that are happening to them and their friends.

Look at current movie and TV program titles, and names of popular musical groups.

Let's Answer This First

Is there an actual Satan? Yes. Satan is an actual spirit being. But, unlike God, Satan can only be one place at a time. He does not have anywhere near the power that God has. Satan is not personally tempting you and me; he is probably off to some more strategic place, meddling in world events. His doom is sealed.

What are demons? We may call them demonic or evil spirits, demons, or refer to them as fallen angels. We don't have to know a lot about them; however, we must realize that we sometimes have to deal with them, and God has given us that authority.

Can Christians have demons? If you had a demon before you were saved, merely asking Jesus into your heart did not evict the evil spirits. They must be cast out verbally, out loud, by a person with strong authority. We hear people argue that demons can't possess you. The "possess" they're talking about is taking total control over your brain to where you're mentally incompetent. Demons cannot possess us but we can possess them in any part of the body.

Can unbelievers be delivered? Yes and No. No usually, since they would have no basis for keeping the evil spirits out. However, I know of some unsaved who were delivered, but then were willing and eager to accept Jesus as Savior after their minds were clear.

What Does the Bible Say?

As you read the New Testament, you can't help but notice that Jesus was tackling evil spirits every time He turned around. Several hundred times the words "spirits," "evil spirits," or "devil," are mentioned in the Scriptures. (See the Appendix to this chapter for a complete list.) That's a lot to be ignoring just because we don't feel like dealing with the subject!

Why are we, who claim belief in the perfection and sanctity of the written Word of God, so hesitant to acknowledge the existence of demons? When we look at the huge amount of biblical statistics concerning demons, how can we deny our responsibility to walk in this obedience? If one-third of the angels fell (Isaiah 14;12, Revelation 12:4), and two-thirds (the good ones) are left in heaven which are counted *"ten thousand times ten thousand"* (100,000,000 = one hundred million) (Revelation 5:11), *"plus thousands of thousands,"* then how many are the one-third that are here on Earth used of Satan to tempt us and/or try to get into us everyday? Zillions!

Demons are ever-present just like the zillions of germs that we understand are everywhere. Get used to them. They only have power if we *give* them power by sin in our life, or if we are unaware of their presence. "So what," we say to the germs. "I can handle them!" A little soap and water and maybe anti-bacterial solutions, and that takes care of them, unless we have some open sores. So let's get used to the idea that we can handle demons just as we have learned to handle germs. Let's stop fearing them as they wish, and demand their obedience to us instead.   Then we would stop being so silly about them and face our everyday fight with demons using the same calm confidence Jesus demonstrated to us, and commanded us to follow.

Why must we fear something we were *given* authority over? If we knew the truth we would not believe the lies. No wonder Satan tries to make us look foolish for believing in demons. No wonder he tries all the tricks of deception.

Not Everyone Wants to Acknowledge the Truth

When I first got involved in delivering people of demons in my little church, I was the first in my community to do so, and there was much scoffing, open criticism, and persecution against us. God had convicted us that if Jesus delivered people from demons and said we should, then we were going to obey Him. The phrase *"Deliverance . . . Anytime"* displayed boldly on the sign outside did not make us popular with the denominational churches. But for those who could not find help with the extraordinary problems like kids hooked on drugs, incurable cancers, unmerciful insanity, and filthy habits that left unbelievers helpless to overcome, we were very popular.

One man came secretly at night for help. He was a pastor of a local church, seeking to get his mentally ill wife delivered from demonic fears beyond his ability to help her. He asked me not to tell anyone, even though she was totally and instantly delivered and healed!

We've found that most of the time cancer is caused by spirits, but not always. It may have to be a deliverance, or it may be a healing.

Elizabeth was a surgical nurse who came for prayer for an entire year without telling me what her problem was; she'd only point to her chest. Finally in desperation I said, "Elizabeth, what is wrong with you? Why don't you tell me?" She finally explained her problem. Both her breasts were as hard as rocks and the pain had gone up in her throat and around to her backbone, and she knew that complete removal of both breasts would not keep her alive. Now that we knew the problem, she was healed in a matter of minutes. The pain gradually left over a period of months, and 15 years later she is alive and well. Without deliverance she would have died.

People who came to our church were desperate for help since they'd tried everything else first. They were finally willing to believe that demons were inflicting them, just as Scripture said. They were relieved to find that there *were* biblical answers to their problems. The solution had been there all along, but was hidden in plain sight.

When I wrote *Don't Be Denied God's Power* with the intent of teaching Christians how to become more mature in their understanding of the power they have over demons, I approached the subject by writing the first chapters about the history of the ineffectiveness of the churches over the ages. *Then*, in the second half of the book, I explained about deliverance from demons.

Not any more! There have been too many more serious devilish problems than people have ever witnessed before, and more and more folks are demanding answers.

Since writing that book, I have found a greater new interest and acceptance by crowds of dear believers who have struggled for so many years, thinking that their own evil hidden personalities were causing their problems. What a relief to find that it was only dumb demons over which Christ gave us the control *if* we would just identify them and cast them out as Christ taught. Their success stories thrilled my heart and spurred me on. They still do.

Psychology and Medicine Have Tried to Answer the Problems

Psychology tries desperately to understand devilish behaviors, but the best they can come up with is to study, identify, and categorize behaviors and try to help people understand themselves and human interactions. The more serious mental illnesses are beyond them, and much too often their patients have to be hidden from society, in hospitals and institutions which are now dangerously full of them. Psychologists and psychiatrists give them names, like psychotics, schizophrenics, manic depressives and other maniacs, and then prescribe drugs to calm them down or pick them up. Sometimes they have some success in trying to change the brain's chemistry with medication, but when you have dealt with as many mentally ill people as we have, you will conclude with us how much dangerous guesswork goes on in that field, and why good-intentioned psychologists have one of the highest suicide rates of all medical professions.

We are glad they were there to help before believers find their authority in Christ Jesus, just the way we appreciate doctors who help folks before they find out how healing and miracles work.

We commend the medical field for their humanitarian efforts. We have worked with some truly dedicated professionals whom we respect, but by their own confessions there is so much more they don't yet understand.

How Did We Miss the Truth?

Satan's strategy is to hide the demons so no one will know they're there. Great tactic of the enemy of our souls! Well, we're not so fooled anymore.

When any denomination tells its people they can't get in you, the demons know where to go and hide. But the Bible says otherwise.

With the many references in our Bible to demons and evil spirits and so many references to our authority and power to overcome them, why are we passive? Because we have been talked out of it? Because we're lazy? Because we're afraid of them? Because we're afraid of what people will say? Because we are afraid that we will fail? *Yes!* to any or all of the above.

Welcome to the club, but we must not be fooled into staying there. We must stay *out* of the "comfortable club" of the Laodicean church which has been lulled into a lukewarm condition, or God says, *"I will spew thee out of my mouth."* (Revelation 3:15,16) Hey, I fight it every day too, especially as I grow older. That's no excuse. Jesus said, *"The kingdom of heaven suffereth violence, and the violent take it [back] by force."* (Matthew 11:12)

This is a fight to take back the kingdom for God from where demons have become comfortably entrenched and do not belong. Cozy, traditional Christianity is not going to get the job done.

Each time I determine to be used of Him to glorify His name by going to deliver some person who calls, I learn more about the subject. We must learn. We must not hold back.

Did Jesus Mean What He Said?

People are hurting, and if we *love* them we must find the help they need — not just be sweet and passive and expect the blessings of God to gently waft down and pamper us in our comfy pews. Jesus said, *"If ye love me, keep my* commandments.*"* (John 14:15, emphasis added) And then He "commanded *them saying ... And as ye go, preach, saying, The kingdom of heaven is at hand. Heal the sick, cleanse the lepers, raise the dead, cast out devils; freely you have received, freely give."* (Matthew 10:5-8)

Was He kidding when He was commanding? Maybe He didn't mean what He said? Maybe He meant the first part and not the last part? Maybe He meant three of those five things, not *all* of them? Maybe this was just a suggestion, an option? No, it was a *command!* It was part of the whole *Great Commission* that the churches claim to be fulfilling. This wasn't written just to the apostles; the proof is found in Matthew 28. The Great Commission was to us all.

Fighting for the lives of those you love is not armchair Christianity. Don't tell them that you love them but you won't help them when their problems embarrass you and make you feel uncomfortable. They need help. They don't merely need your compassion, but your real love. Jesus *loved* those who were having troubles with demons *enough* to heal or deliver them with His overcoming authority, and so must we.

It's our commanded job, and He would not ask us to do what would be impossible to us. Did you really read that list?

1. Preach the gospel,
2. heal the sick,
3. cleanse the lepers,
4. raise the dead,
5. cast out demons. (Matthew 10:8)

We obey only one or two out of the *five*, and think we're being pleasing and obedient to God. Love isn't easy feelings of compassion, it's being effective with the *right* kind of help where it is needed, no matter how awkward it may be to learn the skills required, or how much others may misunderstand.

Do we look at God's written will for us "*to be conformed to the image of his dear Son that he might be the firstborn among many brethren,*" (Romans 8:29), and then say, "but not *that* part of "*his likeness* where He cast out demons from people who needed God's powerful hand which we *all* now have access to?" We must stop that! Growing up in Christ means to be willing to do *all* of God's will, not just the part which is the most comfortable for *us*, and doctrinally correct according to man's theology.

Demons Must Obey the Command of Authority

Stephanie, Bonnie, and May each had awful demonic experiences that would not have happened if they had just been taught to speak out loud to the demons before they were too strong for them to refuse.

Stephanie was brought to us straight from the mental hospital, her eighth incarceration there for suicide attempts. She said, "And I know I will do it again." I delivered her, and two years later she was still free.

Bonnie had been gradually taken over by demons until she said that when she looked in a mirror she saw holes in her forehead, with snakes going in and out of them. The asylum said that if she came again it would be a permanent committal. I ministered deliverance to her, finding that her key demonic spirit was a homosexual one, although she was married and had a child. After her deliverance she was totally normal.

May came to us from New Jersey suffering unsubstantiated pain in many parts of her body. Exploratory surgery revealed absolutely nothing. She was about to be committed to an institution for hallucinating non-existing pains. When I ministered to her she said that every place where I laid my hands on her and told the demons to go was exactly where the pains had been. She was ecstatic to find she didn't have to live with pain any more.

Where would these women be today if they had not learned the truth about speaking aloud to demons? How many more are there out there who are being told that they are just crazy and there is nothing the church can do for them? Where is our responsibility? Are we not going to be held accountable when Jesus said to cast out their demons? What about Matthew 10:8, Matthew 28, and Mark 18 that commands the church to do these things *along with* salvation?

This doesn't mean we're obsessed with "finding demons behind every tree and rock." Many physicians made fun of Florence Nightingale (1820–1910) for claiming that germs were causing infections. She fought for what she knew was right and proved her "theory" about the necessity of washing off germs which were everywhere. Let the church do the same with demons!

Whole denominations have been built on only the Scriptures about salvation, and that was a good start.

But those same denominations pass up the overwhelming number of scriptures dealing with demons.

Who is behind this? Who would benefit most to make us blind to this responsibility but Satan? Let's not be ignorant of his devices by letting this enemy keep us asleep or lazy in this area.

> *But the Lord is faithful, who shall stablish you, and keep you from evil. And we have confidence in the Lord touching you, that ye both do and will do the things which we command you.* [There's that *command* word again!]
>
> (2 Thessalonians 3:3,4)

Step out with this confidence in the Lord's ability to teach you these things He has commanded you to do.

Chapters seven, eight, and Nine of *Don't Be Denied God's Power* are full of the things we successfully learned in our church about delivering folks from demons for more than 30 years. But in this sequel, especially in the next chapter, I have added what we have learned in the seven years since then.

Is This Dangerous Information?

Before going on to the next chapter read all the verses here that refer to Satan and his demons so that you will get a real biblical, godly perspective of what God wants us to know. See for yourself what Scripture says about the reality of the demonic forces which He has asked us to overcome. We were made to have the character of Christ and, thereby, have victory over this prince of the power of the air. We should not be ignorant of the devil's devices. We should have no fear of knowing everything about demons and their strategies.

Some unknowledgeable folks say that reading about the devil gives him too much attention and power. That is as ridiculous as saying that the navy should not do surveillance over enemy territory before it goes to bomb specific ammunition sites and military installations.

How Can I Do This?

God has provided all you need—everything you need to believe, everything you need to do. The Holy Spirit will make you bold and effective in spiritual warfare.

By reading these scriptures, you will not only see the enemy and his army for who they really are. But, most importantly, you will see what God says about how to handle them.

You will gain great insight into the wonderful provisions God has given us with which to become the trained warriors He has predestined us to become in Christ Jesus.

The Bible will prepare you well to fight the good fight of faith with the Word of God, the sword of the Spirit.

It will boost your faith by convincing and convicting you of how much God has spoken of the enemy, expecting us to be aware of his stupid wiles. (Ephesians 6)

It will perfect your mental skills about how to quench all his flaming darts which are attacking your family and friends who are counting on you to help them fight this enemy.

It will make you desire to be more bold as you recall that it was God's idea, not man's, that you possess and use the whole armor of God, and not back down against anything that comes against you.

It will renew your mind about how clear God made it that *He* has given you this predestined offense position, as opposed to just a defensive position.

It will increase your personal knowledge of who you think you are in Christ to be contending against the rulers of this present darkness that continuously present themselves in the nightly news, daily headlines, doctors' reports, and police reports about your neighborhoods. Demons want to scare you to death, but these scriptures will encourage you to be bold and use the weapons of your warfare effectively against them.

Read on, dear Bride, and be perfected. *"Be strong in the Lord and the power of His might that you may be able to stand against the wiles of the devil. "* (Ephesians 6:10,11)

Remember, as I said earlier, don't fall for the pleading of the blood that many churches are into now; it is unscriptural and totally worthless. Power is not in words, it is in the authority Jesus gives.

* * *

Scriptures about devils and Satan—listed by the words, and then in order of appearance in Scripture in the King James Version. Other versions have used different words or phases, but they still have the same meaning. (Italics added by author.)

I.	devils......................................	55
II.	evil spirits..............................	4
III.	unclean spirits........................	10
IV.	familiar spirits........................	9
V.	other spirits............................	2
VI.	seducing spirits........................	1
VII.	spirits...................................	2
VIII.	foul spirit.............................	2
IX.	his (Satan's) angels..................	2
X.	devil....................................	59
	(asterisked ones are not the devil)	
XI.	Dragon..................................	12
XII.	Beelzebub..............................	7
XIII.	serpent.................................	12
XIV.	Accuser.................................	1
XV.	Satan....................................	49
XVI.	Satan's.................................	1
XVII.	prince of the power of the air.......	1
XVIII.	prince of the devils..................	3
XIX.	prince of this world	3
XX.	rulers of the darkness of this world......	1
XXI.	Beast	44
XXII.	Necromancer...........................	2
XXIII.	Wizards.................................	11

I. Devils - 55 times

1. Leviticus 17:7, And they shall no more offer their sacrifices unto *devils*, after whom they have gone a whoring. This shall be a statute forever unto them throughout their generations.

2. Deuteronomy 32:17, They sacrificed unto *devils*, not to God; to gods whom they knew not, to new gods that came newly up, whom your fathers feared not.

3. 2 Chronicles 11:15, And he ordained him priests for the high places, and for the *devils*, and for the calves which he had made.

4. Psalm 106:37, Yea, they sacrificed their sons and their daughters unto *devils*,

5. Matthew 4:24, And his fame went throughout all Syria: and they brought unto him all sick people that were taken with divers diseases and torments, and those which were possessed with *devils*, and those which were lunatic, and those that had the palsy; and he healed them.

6. Matthew 7:22, Many will say to me in that day, Lord, Lord, have we not prophesied in thy name? and in thy name have cast out *devils*? and in thy name done many wonderful works?

7. Matthew 8:16, When the even was come, they brought unto him many that were possessed with *devils*: and he cast out the spirits with his word, and healed all that were sick:

8. Matthew 8:28, And when he was come to the other side into the country of the Gergesenes, there met him two possessed with *devils*, coming out of the tombs, exceeding fierce, so that no man might pass by that way.

9. Matthew 8:31, So the *devils* besought him, saying, If thou cast us out, suffer us to go away into the herd of swine.

10. Matthew 8:33, And they that kept them fled, and went their ways into the city, and told every thing, and what was befallen to the possessed of the *devils*.

11,12. Matthew 9:34, But the Pharisees said, He casteth out *devils* through the prince of the *devils*.

13. Matthew 10:8, Heal the sick, cleanse the lepers, raise the dead, cast out *devils*: freely ye have received, freely give.

14,15. Matthew 12:24, But when the Pharisees heard it, they said, This fellow doth not cast out *devils*, but by Beelzebub the prince of the *devils*.

16. Matthew 12:27, And if I by Beelzebub cast out *devils*, by whom do your children cast them out? Therefore, they shall be your judges.

17. Matthew 12:28, But if I cast out *devils* by the Spirit of God, then the kingdom of God is come unto you.

18. Mark 1:32, And at even, when the sun did set, they brought unto him all that were diseased, and them that were possessed with *devils*.

19,20. Mark 1:34, And he healed many that were sick of divers diseases, and cast out many *devils*; and suffered not the *devils* to speak, because they knew him.

21. Mark 1:39, And he preached in their synagogues throughout all Galilee, and cast out *devils*.

22. Mark 3:15, And to have power to heal sicknesses, and to cast out *devils*.

23,24. Mark 3:22, And the scribes which came down from Jerusalem said, He hath Beelzebub, and by the prince of the *devils* casteth he out *devils*.

25. Mark 5:12, And all the *devils* besought him, saying, Send us into the swine, that we may enter into them.

26. Mark 6:13, And they cast out many *devils*, and anointed with oil many that were sick, and healed them.

27. Mark 9:38, And John answered him, saying, Master, we saw one casting out *devils* in thy name, and he followeth not us: and we forbade him, because he followeth not us.

28. Mark 16:9, Now when Jesus was risen early the first day of the week, he appeared first to Mary Magdalene, out of whom he had cast seven *devils*.

29. Mark 16:17, And these signs shall follow them that believe; In my name shall they cast out *devils*; they shall speak with new tongues.

30. Luke 4:41, And *devils* also came out of many, crying out, and saying, Thou art Christ the Son of God. And he rebuking them, suffered them not to speak: for they knew that he was Christ.

31. Luke 8:2, And certain women, which had been healed of evil spirits and infirmities, Mary called Magdalene, out of whom went seven *devils*.

32. Luke 8:27, And when he went forth to land, there met him out of the city a certain man, which had *devils* for a long time, and wore no clothes, neither abode in any house, but in the tombs.

33. Luke 8:30, And Jesus asked him, saying, What is thy name? And he said, Legion: because many *devils* were entered into him.

34. Luke 8:33, Then went the *devils* out of the man, and entered into the swine: and the herd ran violently down a steep place into the lake, and were choked.

35. Luke 8:35, Then they went out to see what was done; and came to Jesus, and found the man, out of whom the *devils* were departed, sitting at the feet of Jesus, clothed, and in his right mind: and they were afraid.

36. Luke 8:36, They also which saw it told them by what means he that was possessed of the *devils* was healed.

37. Luke 8:38, Now the man out of whom the *devils* were departed besought him that he might be with him: but Jesus sent him away.

38. Luke 9:1, Then he called his twelve disciples together, and gave them power and authority over all *devils*, and to cure diseases.

39. Luke 9:49, And John answered and said, Master, we saw one casting out *devils* in thy name; and we forbade him, because he followeth not with us.

40. Luke 10:17, And the seventy returned again with joy, saying, Lord, even the *devils* are subject unto us through thy name.

41,42. Luke 11:15, But some of them said, He casteth out *devils* through Beelzebub the chief of the *devils*.

43. Luke 11:18, If Satan also be divided against himself, how shall his kingdom stand? because ye say that I cast out *devils* through Beelzebub.

44. Luke 11:19, And if I by Beelzebub cast out *devils*, by whom do your sons cast them out? therefore shall they be your judges.

45. Luke 11:20, But if I with the finger of God cast out *devils*, no doubt the kingdom of God is come upon you.

46. Luke 13:32, And he said unto them, Go ye, and tell that fox, Behold, I cast out *devils*, and I do cures to day and to morrow, and the third day I shall be perfected.

47,48. 1 Corinthians 10:20, But I say, that the things which the Gentiles sacrifice, they sacrifice to *devils*, and not to God: and I would not that ye should have fellowship with *devils*.

49,50. 1 Corinthians 10:21, Ye cannot drink the cup of the Lord, and the cup of *devils*: ye cannot be partakers of the Lord's table, and of the table of *devils*.

51. 1 Timothy 4:1, Now the Spirit speaketh expressly, that in the latter times some shall depart from the faith, giving heed to seducing spirits, and doctrines of *devils*.

52. James 2:19, Thou believest that there is one God; thou doest well: the *devils* also believe, and tremble.

53. Revelation 9:20, And the rest of the men which were not killed by these plagues yet repented not of the works of their hands, that they should not worship *devils*, and idols of gold, and silver, and brass, and stone, and of wood: which neither can see, nor hear, nor walk.

54. Revelation 16:14, For they are the spirits of *devils*, working miracles, which go forth unto the kings of the earth and of the whole world, to gather them to the battle of that great day of God Almighty.

55. (Revelation 18:2, And he cried mightily with a strong voice, saying, Babylon the great is fallen, is fallen, and is become the habitation of *devils*, and the hold of every foul spirit, and a cage of every unclean and hateful bird.

II. Evil Spirits, 4 times

1. Luke 7:21, And in that same hour he cured many of their infirmities and plagues, and of *evil spirits*; and unto many [that were] blind he gave sight.

2. Luke 8:2, And certain women, which had been healed of *evil spirits* and infirmities, Mary called Magdalene, out of whom went seven devils,

3. Acts 19:12, So that from his body were brought unto the sick handkerchiefs or aprons, and the diseases departed from them, and the *evil spirits* went out of them.

4. Acts 19:13, Then certain of the vagabond Jews, exorcists, took upon them to call over them which had *evil spirits* the name of the Lord Jesus, saying, We adjure you by Jesus whom Paul preaches.

III. Unclean Spirits, 10 times

1. Matthew 10:1, And when he had called unto him his twelve disciples, he gave them power against *unclean spirits*, to cast them out, and to heal all manner of sickness and all manner of disease.

2. Mark 1:27, And they were all amazed, insomuch that they questioned among themselves, saying, What thing is this? what new doctrine is this? For with authority commandeth he even the *unclean spirits*, and they do obey him.

3. Mark 3:11, And *unclean spirits*, when they saw him, fell down before him, and cried, saying, Thou art the Son of God.

4. Mark 5:13, And forthwith Jesus gave them leave. And the *unclean spirits* went out, and entered into the swine: and the herd ran violently down a steep place into the sea, (they were about two thousand;) and were choked in the sea.

5. Mark 6:7, And he called unto him the twelve, and began to send them forth by two and two; and gave them power over *unclean spirits*.

6. Luke 4:36, And they were all amazed, and spake among themselves, saying, What a word is this! for with authority and power he commandeth the *unclean spirits*, and they come out.

7. Luke 6:18, And they that were vexed with *unclean spirits*: and they were healed.

8. Acts 5:16, There came also a multitude out of the cities round about unto Jerusalem, bringing sick folks, and them which were vexed with *unclean spirits*: and they were healed every one.

9. Acts 8:7, For *unclean spirits*, crying with a loud voice, came out of many that were possessed with them: and many taken with palsies, and that were lame, were healed.

10. Revelation 16:13, And I saw the *unclean spirits* like frogs come out of the mouth of the dragon, and out of the mouth of the beast, and out of the mouth of the false prophet.

IV. Familiar Spirits, 9 times (used in Old Testament)

1. Leviticus 19:31, Regard not them that have *familiar spirits*, neither seek after wizards, to be defiled by them: I am the LORD your God.

2. Leviticus 20:6, And the soul that turneth after such as have *familiar spirits*, and after wizards, to go a whoring after them, I will even set my face against that soul, and will cut him off from among his people.

3. Deuteronomy 18:11, Or a charmer, or a consulter with *familiar spirits*, or a wizard, or a necromancer.

4. 1 Samuel 28:3, Now Samuel was dead, and all Israel had lamented him, and buried him in Ramah, even in his own city. And Saul had put away those that had *familiar spirits*, and the wizards, out of the land.

5. 1 Samuel 28:9, And the woman said unto him, Behold, thou knowest what Saul hath done, how he hath cut off those that have *familiar spirits*, and the wizards, out of the land: wherefore then layest thou a snare for my life, to cause me to die?

6. 2 Kings 21:6, And he made his son pass through the fire, and observed times, and used enchantments, and dealt with *familiar spirits* and wizards: he wrought much wickedness in the sight of the LORD, to provoke him to anger.

7. 2 Kings 23:24, Moreover, the workers with *familiar spirits*, and the wizards, and the images, and the idols, and all the abominations that were spied in the land of Judah and in Jerusalem, did Josiah put away, that he might perform the words of the law which were written in the book that Hilkiah the priest found in the house of the LORD.

8. Isaiah 8:19, And when they shall say unto you, Seek unto them that have *familiar spirits*, and unto wizards that peep, and that mutter: should not a people seek unto their God? for the living to the dead?

9. Isaiah 19:3, And the spirit of Egypt shall fail in the midst thereof; and I will destroy the counsel thereof: and they shall seek to the idols, and to the charmers, and to them that have *familiar spirits*, and to the wizards.

V. Other Spirits, wicked, 2 times

1. Matthew 12:45, Then goeth he, and taketh with himself seven *other spirits* more *wicked* than himself, and they enter in and dwell there: and the last state of that man is worse than the first. Even so shall it be also unto this wicked generation.

2. Luke 11:26, Then goeth he, and taketh to him seven *other spirits* more *wicked* than himself; and they enter in, and dwell there: and the last state of that man is worse than the first.

VI. Seducing Spirits, 1 time

1. 1 Timothy 4:1, Now the Spirit speaketh expressly, that in the latter times some shall depart from the faith, giving heed to *seducing spirits*, and doctrines of devils.

VII. Spirits, 2 times

1. Luke 10:20, Notwithstanding in this rejoice not, that the *spirits* are subject unto you; but rather rejoice because your names are written in heaven.

2. 1 Corinthians 12:10, To another the working of miracles; to another prophecy; to another discerning of *spirits*, to another divers kinds of tongues, to another the interpretation of tongues.

VIII. Foul Spirit, 2 times

1. Mark 9:25, When Jesus saw that the people came running together, he rebuked the *foul spirit,* saying unto him Thou dumb and deaf spirit, I charge thee, come out of him, and enter no more into him.

2. Revelation 18:2, And he cried mightily with a strong voice, saying, Babylon the great is fallen, is fallen, and is become the habitation of devils, and the hold of every *foul spirit,* and a cage of every unclean and hateful bird.

IX.   His (Satan's) Angels, 2 times

1.) Matthew. 25:41, Then shall he say unto them on the left hand, Depart from me, ye cursed, into everlasting fire, prepared for the devil and *his angels.*

2. Psalm 78:49, He cast upon them the fierceness of his anger, wrath, and indignation, and trouble, by sending *evil angels* among them.

X. Devil, 59 times (sometimes referring to the devil, and sometimes referring to the particular devil in a person— pointed out with an asterisk *)

1. Matthew 4:1, Then was Jesus led up of the Spirit into the wilderness to be tempted of *the devil.*

2. Matthew 4:5, Then *the devil* taketh him up into the holy city, and setteth him on a pinnacle of the temple,

3. Matthew 4:8, Again, *the devil* taketh him up into an exceeding high mountain, and sheweth him all the kingdoms of the world, and the glory of them.

4. Matthew 4:11, Then *the devil* leaveth him, and, behold, angels came and ministered unto him.

5. *Matthew 9:32, As they went out, behold, they brought to him a dumb man possessed with *a devil.*

6. *Matthew 9:33, And when *the devil* was cast out, the dumb spake: and the multitudes marveled, saying, It was never so seen in Israel.

7. *Matthew 11:18, For John came neither eating nor drinking, and they say, He hath *a devil.*

8. *Matthew 12:22, Then was brought unto him one possessed with *a devil,* blind, and dumb: and he healed him, insomuch that the blind and dumb both spake and saw.

9. *Matthew 13:39, The enemy that sowed them is *the devil;* the harvest is the end of the world; and the reapers are the angels.

10. *Matthew 15:22, And, behold, a woman of Canaan came out of the same coasts, and cried unto him, saying, Have mercy on me, O Lord, thou Son of David; my daughter is grievously vexed with *a devil.*

11. *Matthew 17:18, And Jesus rebuked *the devil;* and he departed out of him: and the child was cured from that very hour.

12. Matthew 25:41, Then shall he say also unto them on the left hand, Depart from me, ye cursed, into everlasting fire, prepared for *the devil* and his angels.

13.* Mark 5:15, And they come to Jesus, and see him that was possessed with *the devil,* and had the legion, sitting, and clothed, and in his right mind: and they were afraid.

14. *Mark 5:16, And they that saw it told them how it befell to him that was possessed with *the devil,* and also concerning the swine.

15. *Mark 5:18, And when he was come into the ship, he that had been possessed with *the devil* prayed him that he might be with him.

16. *Mark 7:26, The woman was a Greek, a Syrophoenician by nation; and she besought him that he would cast forth *the devil* out of her daughter.

17. *Mark 7:29, And he said unto her, For this saying go thy way; *the devil* is gone out of thy daughter.

18. *Mark 7:30, And when she was come to her house, she found *the devil* gone out, and her daughter laid upon the bed.

19. Luke 4:2, Being forty days tempted of *the devil.* And in those days he did eat nothing: and when they were ended, he afterward hungered.

20. Luke 4:3, And *the devil* said unto him, If thou be the Son of God, command this stone that it be made bread.

21. Luke 4:5, And *the devil,* taking him up into an high mountain, showed unto him all the kingdoms of the world in a moment of time.

22. Luke 4:6, And *the devil* said unto him, All this power will I give thee, and the glory of them: for that is delivered unto me; and to whomsoever I will give it.

23. Luke 4:9, And *he [the devil]* brought him to Jerusalem, and set him on a pinnacle of the temple, and said unto him, If thou be the Son of God, cast thyself down from hence:

24. Luke 4:13 And when *the devil* had ended all the temptation, he departed from him for a season.

25.* Luke 4:33, And in the synagogue there was a man, which had a spirit of an *unclean devil,* and cried out with a loud voice,

26. Luke 4:35, And Jesus rebuked him, saying, Hold thy peace, and come out of him. And when *the devil* had thrown him in the midst, he came out of him, and hurt him not.

27.* Luke 7:33, For John the Baptist came neither eating bread nor drinking wine; and ye say, He hath *a devil.*

28. Luke 8:12, Those by the way side are they that hear; then cometh *the devil,* and taketh away the word out of their hearts, lest they should believe and be saved.

29. * Luke 8:29, (For he had commanded the unclean spirit to come out of the man. For oftentimes it had caught him: and he was kept bound with chains and in fetters; and he brake the bands, and was driven of *the devil* into the wilderness.)

30. * Luke 9:42, And as he was coming, *the devil* threw him down, and tore him. And Jesus rebuked the unclean spirit, and healed the child, and delivered him again to his father.

31. *Luke 11:14, And he was casting out *a devil,* and it was dumb. And it came to pass, when *the devil* was gone out, the dumb spake; and the people wondered.

32. John 6:70, Jesus answered them, Have not I chosen you twelve, and one of you is *a devil?*

33. *John 7:20, The people answered and said, Thou hast *a devil:* who goeth about to kill thee?

34. John 8:44, Ye are of your father *the devil,* and the lusts of your father ye will do. He was a murderer from the beginning, and abode not in the truth, because there is no truth in him. When he speaketh a lie, he speaketh of his own: for he is a liar, and the father of it.

35.* John 8:48, Then answered the Jews, and said unto him, Say we not well that thou art a Samaritan, and hast *a devil?*

36.* John 8:49, Jesus answered, I have not *a devil;* but I honor my Father, and ye do dishonor me.

37.* John 8:52, Then said the Jews unto him, Now we know that thou hast *a devil.* Abraham is dead, and the prophets; and thou sayest, If a man keep my saying, he shall never taste of death.

38.* John 10:20, And many of them said, He hath *a devil,* and is mad; why hear ye him?

39. *John 10:21, Others said, These are not the words of him that hath *a devil.* Can *a devil* open the eyes of the blind?

40. John 13:2, And supper being ended, *the devil* having now put into the heart of Judas Iscariot, Simon's son, to betray him;

41. Acts 10:38, How God anointed Jesus of Nazareth with the Holy Ghost and with power: who went about doing good, and healing all that were oppressed of *the devil;* for God was with him.

42. Acts 13:10, And said, O full of all subtlety and all mischief, thou child of *the devil,* thou enemy of all righteousness, wilt thou not cease to pervert the right ways of the Lord?

43. Ephesians 4:27, Neither give place to *the devil.*

44. Ephesians 6:11, Put on the whole armor of God, that ye may be able to stand against the wiles of *the devil.*

45. 1 Timothy 3:6, Not a novice, lest being lifted up with pride he fall into the condemnation of *the devil.*

46. 1 Timothy 3:7, Moreover he must have a good report of them which are without; lest he fall into reproach and the snare of *the devil.*

47. 2 Timothy 2:26, And that they may recover themselves out of the snare of *the devil,* who are taken captive by him at his will.

48. Hebrews 2:14, Forasmuch then as the children are partakers of flesh and blood, he also himself likewise took part of the same; that through death he might destroy him that had the power of death, that is, *the devil.*

49. James 3:15, This wisdom descends not from above, but is earthly, sensual, *devilish.*

50. James 4:7, Submit yourselves therefore to God. Resist *the devil,* and he will flee from you.

51. 1 Peter 5:8, Be sober, be vigilant; because your adversary *the devil,* as a roaring lion, walks about, seeking whom he may devour.

52. 1 John 3:8, He that committeth sin is of *the devil;* for *the devil* sinneth from the beginning. For this purpose the Son of God was manifested, that he might destroy the works of *the devil.*

3:10, In this the children of God are
e children of *the devil:* whosoever doeth not
is not of God, neither he that loveth not his

de 1:9, Yet Michael the archangel, when
contending with *the devil* he disputed about the body of
Moses, dared not bring against him a railing accusation, but
said, The Lord rebuke thee.

55. Revelation 2:10, Fear none of those things which
thou shalt suffer: behold, *the devil* shall cast some of you
into prison, that ye may be tried; and ye shall have tribulation
ten days: be thou faithful unto death, and I will give thee a
crown of life.

56. Revelation 12:9, And the great dragon was cast
out, that old serpent, called *the Devil* and Satan, which
deceiveth the whole world: he was cast out into the earth,
and his angels were cast out with him.

57. Revelation 12:12, Therefore rejoice, ye heavens,
and ye that dwell in them. Woe to the inhabiters of the earth
and of the sea! For *the devil* is come down unto you, having
great wrath, because he knoweth that he hath but a short
time.

58. Revelation 20:2, And he laid hold on the dragon,
that old serpent, which is *the Devil,* and Satan, and bound
him a thousand years.

59. Revelation 20:10, And *the devil* that deceived them
was cast into the lake of fire and brimstone, where the beast
and the false prophet are, and shall be tormented day and
night for ever and ever.

XI. Dragon, Referring to Satan, 12 times

1. Revelation 12:3, And there appeared another wonder
in heaven; and behold a great red *dragon,* having seven
heads and ten horns, and seven crowns upon his heads.

2. Revelation 12:4, And his tail drew the third part of the stars of heaven, and did cast them to the earth: and the *dragon* stood before the woman which was ready to be delivered, for to devour her child as soon as it was born.

3. Revelation 12:7, And there was war in heaven: Michael and his angels fought against the *dragon;* and the dragon fought and his angels.

4. Revelation 12:9, And the great *dragon* was cast out, that old serpent, called the Devil, and Satan, which deceiveth the whole world: he was cast out into the earth, and his angels were cast out with him.

5. Revelation 12:13, And when the *dragon* saw that he was cast unto the earth, he persecuted the woman which brought forth the man child.

6. Revelation 12:16, And the earth helped the woman, and the earth opened her mouth, and swallowed up the flood which the *dragon* cast out of his mouth.

7. Revelation 12:17, And the *dragon* was wroth with the woman, and went to make war with the remnant of her seed, which keep the commandments of God, and have the testimony of Jesus Christ.

8. Revelation 13:2, And the beast which I saw was like unto a leopard, and his feet were as the feet of a bear, and his mouth as the mouth of a lion: and the *dragon* gave him his power, and his seat, and great authority.

9. Revelation 13:4, And they worshiped the *dragon* which gave power unto the beast: and they worshiped the beast, saying, Who is like unto the beast? Who is able to make war with him?

10. Revelation 13:11, And I beheld another beast coming up out of the earth; and he had two horns like a lamb, and he spake as a *dragon.*

11. Revelation 16:13, And I saw there unclean spirits like frogs come out of the mouth of the *dragon,* and out of the mouth of the beast, and out of the mouth of the false prophet.

12. Revelation 20:2, And he laid hold on the *dragon,* that old serpent, which is the Devil, and Satan, and bound him a thousand years.

XII. Beelzebub, 7 times

1. Matthew 10:25, It is enough for the disciple that he be as his master, and the servant as his lord. If they have called the master of the house *Beelzebub,* how much more shall they call them of his household?

2. Matthew 12:24, But when the Pharisees heard it, they said, This fellow doth not cast out devils, but by *Beelzebub* the prince of the devils.

3. Matthew 12:27, And if I by *Beelzebub* cast out devils, by whom do your children cast them out? therefore they shall be your judges.

4. Mark 3:22, And the scribes which came down from Jerusalem said, He hath *Beelzebub*, and by the prince of the devils casteth he out devils.

5. Luke 11:15, But some of them said, He casteth out devils through *Beelzebub* the chief of the devils.

6. Luke 11:18, If Satan also be divided against himself, how shall his kingdom stand? because ye say that I cast out devils through *Beelzebub*.

7. Luke 11:19, And if I by *Beelzebub* cast out devils, by whom do your sons cast them out? Therefore, shall they be your judges.

XIII. The Serpent (meaning Satan), 12 times

1. Genesis 3:1, Now *the serpent* was more subtle than any beast of the field which the LORD God had made. And he said unto the woman, Yea, hath God said, Ye shall not eat of every tree of the garden?

2. Genesis 3:2, And the woman said unto *the serpent*, We may eat of the fruit of the trees of the garden.

3. Genesis 3:4, And *the serpent* said unto the woman, Ye shall not surely die.

4. Genesis 3:13, And the LORD God said unto the woman, What is this that thou hast done? And the woman said, *The serpent* beguiled me, and I did eat.

5. Genesis 3:14, And the LORD God said unto *the serpent*, Because thou hast done this, thou art cursed above all cattle, and above every beast of the field; upon thy belly shalt thou go, and dust shalt thou eat all the days of thy life:

6. Isaiah 14:29, Rejoice not thou, whole Palestina, because the rod of him that smote thee is broken: for out of *the serpent's* root shall come forth a cockatrice, and his fruit shall be a fiery flying serpent.

7. Isaiah 27:1, In that day the LORD with his sore and great and strong sword shall punish Leviathan the piercing *serpent,* even Leviathan that crooked *serpent;* and he shall slay the dragon that is in the sea.

8. 2 Corinthians 11:3, But I fear, lest by any means, as *the serpent* beguiled Eve through his subtlety, so your minds should be corrupted from the simplicity that is in Christ.

9. Revelation 12:9, And the great dragon was cast out, that old *serpent,* called the Devil, and Satan, which deceiveth the whole world: he was cast out into the earth, and his angels were cast out with him.

10. Revelation 12:14, And to the woman were given two wings of a great eagle, that she might fly into the wilderness, into her place, where she is nourished for a time, and times, and half a time, from the face of *the serpent*.

11. Revelation 12:15, And *the serpent* cast out of his mouth water as a flood after the woman, that he might cause her to be carried away of the flood.

12. Revelation 20:2, And he laid hold on the dragon, that old *serpent,* which is the Devil, and Satan, and bound him a thousand years,

XIV. The Accuser, 1 time

Revelation 12:10, And I heard a loud voice saying in heaven, Now is come salvation, and strength, and the kingdom of our God, and the power of his Christ: for the *Accuser* of our brethren is cast down, which accused them before our God day and night.

XV. Satan, 49 times

1. 1 Chronicles 21:1, And *Satan* stood up against Israel, and provoked David to number Israel.

2. Job 1:6, Now there was a day when the sons of God came to present themselves before the LORD, and *Satan* came also among them.

3. Job 1:7, And the LORD said unto *Satan,* Whence comest thou? Then *Satan* answered the LORD, and said, From going to and fro in the earth, and from walking up and down in it.

4. Job 1:8, And the LORD said unto *Satan,* Hast thou considered my servant Job, that there is none like him in the earth, a perfect and an upright man, one that feareth God, and escheweth evil?

5. Job 1:9, Then *Satan* answered the LORD, and said, Doth Job fear God for nought?

6. Job 1:12, And the LORD said unto *Satan,* Behold, all that he hath is in thy power; only upon himself put not forth thine hand. So *Satan* went forth from the presence of the LORD.

7. Job 2:1, Again there was a day when the sons of God came to present themselves before the LORD, and *Satan* came also among them to present himself before the LORD.

8. Job 2:2, And the LORD said unto Satan, From whence comest thou? And *Satan* answered the LORD, and said, From going to and fro in the earth, and from walking up and down in it.

9. Job 2:3, And the LORD said unto *Satan*, Hast thou considered my servant Job, that there is none like him in the earth, a perfect and an upright man, one that feareth God, and escheweth evil? and still he holdeth fast his integrity, although thou movedst me against him, to destroy him without cause.

10. Job 2:4, And *Satan* answered the LORD, and said, Skin for skin, yea, all that a man hath will he give for his life.

11. Job 2:6, And the LORD said unto *Satan,* Behold, he is in thine hand; but save his life.

12. Job 2:7, So went *Satan* forth from the presence of the LORD, and smote Job with sore boils from the sole of his foot unto his crown.

13. Psalm 109:6, Set thou a wicked man over him: and let *Satan* stand at his right hand.

14. Zechariah 3:1, And he shewed me Joshua the high priest standing before the angel of the LORD, and *Satan* standing at his right hand to resist him.

15. Zechariah 3:2, And the LORD said unto *Satan*, The LORD rebuke thee, O *Satan;* even the LORD that hath chosen Jerusalem rebuke thee: is not this a brand plucked out of the fire?

16. Matthew 4:10, Then saith Jesus unto him, Get thee hence, <u>Satan</u>: for it is written, Thou shalt worship the Lord thy God, and him only shalt thou serve.

17. Matthew 12:26, And if <u>Satan</u> cast out <u>Satan</u>, he is divided against himself; how shall then his kingdom stand?

18. Matthew 16:23, But he turned, and said unto Peter, Get thee behind me, *Satan*: thou art an offence unto me: for thou savourest not the things that be of God, but those that be of men.

19. Mark 1:13, And he was there in the wilderness forty days, tempted of *Satan*; and was with the wild beasts; and the angels ministered unto him.

20. Mark 3:23, And he called them unto him, and said unto them in parables, How can *Satan* cast out *Satan*?

21. Mark 3:26, And if *Satan* rise up against himself, and be divided, he cannot stand, but hath an end.

22. Mark 4:15, And these are they by the way side, where the word is sown; but when they have heard, *Satan* cometh immediately, and taketh away the word that was sown in their hearts.

23. Mark 8:33, But when he had turned about and looked on his disciples, he rebuked Peter, saying, Get thee behind me, *Satan*: for thou savourest not the things that be of God, but the things that be of men.

24. Luke 4:8, And Jesus answered and said unto him, Get thee behind me, *Satan*: for it is written, Thou shalt worship the Lord thy God, and him only shalt thou serve.

25. Luke 10:18, And he said unto them, I beheld *Satan* as lightning fall from heaven.

26. Luke 11:18, If *Satan* also be divided against himself, how shall his kingdom stand? because ye say that I cast out devils through Beelzebub.

27. Luke 13:16, And ought not this woman, being a daughter of Abraham, whom *Satan* hath bound, lo, these eighteen years, be loosed from this bond on the sabbath day?

28. Luke 22:3, Then entered *Satan* into Judas surnamed Iscariot, being of the number of the twelve.

29. Luke 22:31, And the Lord said, Simon, Simon, behold, *Satan* hath desired to have you, that he may sift you as wheat.

30. John 13:27, And after the sop *Satan* entered into him. Then said Jesus unto him, That thou doest, do quickly.

31. Acts 5:3, But Peter said, Ananias, why hath *Satan* filled thine heart to lie to the Holy Ghost, and to keep back part of the price of the land?

32. Acts 26:18, To open their eyes, and to turn them from darkness to light, and from the power of *Satan* unto God, that they may receive forgiveness of sins, and inheritance among them which are sanctified by faith that is in me.

33. Romans 16:20, And the God of peace shall bruise *Satan* under your feet shortly. The grace of our Lord Jesus Christ be with you. Amen.

34. 1 Corinthians 5:5, To deliver such an one unto *Satan* for the destruction of the flesh, that the spirit may be saved in the day of the Lord Jesus.

35. 1 Corinthians 7:5, Defraud ye not one the other, except it be with consent for a time, that ye may give yourselves to fasting and prayer; and come together again, that *Satan* tempt you not for your incontinency.

36. 2 Corinthians 2:11, Lest *Satan* should get an advantage of us: for we are not ignorant of his devices.

37. 2 Corinthians 11:14, And no marvel; for *Satan* himself is transformed into an angel of light.

38. 2 Corinthians 12:7, And lest I should be exalted above measure through the abundance of the revelations, there was given to me a thorn in the flesh, the messenger of *Satan* to buffet me, lest I should be exalted above measure.

39. 1 Thessalonians 2:18, Wherefore we would have come unto you, even I Paul, once and again; but *Satan* hindered us.

40. 2 Thessalonians 2:9, Even him, whose coming is after the working of *Satan* with all power and signs and lying wonders.

41. 1 Timothy 1:20, Of whom is Hymenaeus and Alexander; whom I have delivered unto *Satan*, that they may learn not to blaspheme.

42. 1 Timothy 5:15, For some are already turned aside after *Satan*.

43. Revelation 2:9, I know thy works, and tribulation, and poverty, (but thou art rich) and I know the blasphemy of them which say they are Jews, and are not, but are the synagogue of *Satan*.

44. Revelation 2:13, I know thy works, and where thou dwellest, even where Satan's seat is: and thou holdest fast my name, and hast not denied my faith, even in those days wherein Antipas was my faithful martyr, who was slain among you, where *Satan* dwelleth.

45. Revelation 2:24, But unto you I say, and unto the rest in Thyatira, as many as have not this doctrine, and which have not known the depths of *Satan*, as they speak; I will put upon you none other burden.

46. Revelation 3:9, Behold, I will make them of the synagogue of *Satan*, which say they are Jews, and are not, but do lie; behold, I will make them to come and worship before thy feet, and to know that I have loved thee.

47. Revelation 12:9, And the great dragon was cast out, that old serpent, called the Devil, and *Satan*, which deceiveth the whole world: he was cast out into the earth, and his angels were cast out with him.

48. Revelation 20:2, And he laid hold on the dragon, that old serpent, which is the Devil and *Satan*, and bound him a thousand years.

49. Revelation 20:7,8, And when the thousand years are expired, *Satan* shall be loosed out of his prison, and shall go out to deceive the nations which are in the four quarters of the earth, Gog and Magog, to gather them together to battle: the number is as the sand of the sea.

XVI. Satan's, 1 time

1. Revelation 2:13, I know thy works, and where thou dwellest, even where *Satan's* seat is: and thou holdest fast my name, and hast not denied my faith, even in those days wherein Antipas was my faithful martyr, who was slain among you, where Satan dwelleth.

XVII. Prince of the Power of the Air, 1 time

1. Ephesians 2:2, Wherein in time past you walked according to the course of this world, according to the *prince of the power of the air*, the spirit that now worketh in the children of disobedience.

XVIII. Prince of the Devils, 3 times

1. Matthew 9:34, But the Pharisees said, He casteth out devils through the *prince of the devils.*
2. Matthew 12:24, But when the Pharisees heard it, they said, This fellow doth not cast out devils, but by Beelzebub the *prince of devils.*
3. Mark 3:22, And the scribes which came down from Jerusalem said, He hath Beelzebub, and by the *prince of devils* casteth he out devils.

XIX. Prince of This World, 3 times

1. John 12:31, Now is the judgment of this world: now shall the *prince of this world* be cast out.
2. John 14:30, Hereafter I will not talk much with you: for the *prince of this world* cometh, and hath nothing in me.
3. John 16:11, Of judgment, because the *prince of this world* is judged.

XX. Rulers of the Darkness of this World, 1 time

1. Ephesians 6:12, For we wrestle not against flesh and blood, but against principalities, against powers, against the *rulers of the darkness of this world*, against spiritual wickedness in high places.

XXI. Beast, 44 mentions in Book of Revelation, in 35 verses. (It doesn't apply to demons.)

1. Revelation 4:7, And the first *beast* was like a lion, and the second *beast* like a calf, and the third *beast* had a face as a man, and the fourth *beast* was like a flying eagle.

2. Revelation 6:3, And when he had opened the second seal, I heard the second *beast* say, Come and see.

3. Revelation 6:5, And when he had opened the third seal, I heard the third *beast* say, Come and see. And I beheld, and lo a black horse; and he that sat on him had a pair of balances in his hand.

4. Revelation 6:7, And when he had opened the fourth seal, I heard the voice of the fourth *beast* say, Come and see.

5. Revelation 11:7, And when they shall have finished their testimony, the *beast* that ascendeth out of the bottomless pit shall make war against them, and shall overcome them, and kill them.

6. Revelation 13:1, And I stood upon the sand of the sea, and saw a *beast* rise up out of the sea, having seven heads and ten horns, and upon his horns ten crowns, and upon his heads the name of blasphemy.

7. Revelation 13:2, And the *beast* which I saw was like unto a leopard, and his feet were as the feet of a bear, and his mouth as the mouth of a lion: and the dragon gave him his power, and his seat, and great authority.

8. Revelation 13:3, And I saw one of his heads as it were wounded to death; and his deadly wound was healed: and all the world wondered after the *beast*.

9. Revelation 13:4, And they worshiped the dragon which gave power unto the *beast*: and they worshiped the *beast*.

10. Revelation 13:5, And there was given unto him a mouth speaking great things and blasphemies; and power was given unto him to continue forty and two months.

11. Revelation 13:8, And all that dwell upon the earth shall worship him, whose names are not written in the book of life of the Lamb slain from the foundation of the world.

12. Revelation 13:11, And I beheld another *beast* coming up out of the earth; and he had two horns like a lamb, and he spake as a dragon.

13. Revelation 13:12, And he exerciseth all the power of the first *beast* before him, and causeth the earth and them which dwell therein to worship the first *beast*, whose deadly wound was healed.

14. Revelation 13:14, And deceiveth them that dwell on the earth by the means of those miracles which he had power to do in the sight of the *beast*; saying to them that dwell on the earth, that they should make an image to the *beast*, which had the wound by a sword, and did live.

15. Revelation 13:15, And he had power to give life unto the image of the *beast*, that the image of the *beast* should both speak, and cause that as many as would not worship the image of the *beast* should be killed.

16. Revelation 13:17, And that no man might buy or sell, save he that had the mark, or the name of the *beast*, or the number of his name.

17. Revelation 13:18, Here is wisdom. Let him that hath understanding count the number of the *beast*: for it is the number of a man; and his number is six hundred threescore and six.

18. Revelation 14:9, And the third angel followed them, saying with a loud voice, If any man worship the *beast* and his image, and receive his mark in his forehead, or in his hand . . .

19. Revelation 14:11, And the smoke of their torment ascendeth up for ever and ever: and they have no rest day nor night, who worship the *beast* and his image.

20. Revelation 15:2, And I saw as it were a sea of glass mingled with fire: and them that had gotten the victory over the *beast*, and over his image, and over his mark, and over the number of his name, stand on the sea of glass, having the harps of God.

21. Revelation 16:2, And the first went, and poured out his vial upon the earth; and there fell a noisome and grievous sore upon the men which had the mark of the *beast*, and upon them which worshiped his image.

22. Revelation 16:10, And the fifth angel poured out his vial upon the seat of the *beast*; and his kingdom was full of darkness; and they gnawed their tongues for pain.

23. Revelation 16:13, And I saw three unclean spirits like frogs come out of the mouth of the dragon, and out of the mouth of the *beast*, and out of the mouth of the false prophet.

24. Revelation 17:3, So he carried me away in the spirit into the wilderness: and I saw a woman sit upon a scarlet colored *beast*, full of names of blasphemy, having seven heads and ten horns.

25. Revelation 17:7, And the angel said unto me, Wherefore didst thou marvel? I will tell thee the mystery of the woman, and of the *beast* that carrieth her, which hath the seven heads and ten horns.

26. Revelation 17:8, The *beast* that thou sawest was, and is not; and shall ascend out of the bottomless pit, and go into perdition: and they that dwell on the earth shall wonder, whose names were not written in the book of life from the foundation of the world, when they behold the *beast* that was, and is not, and yet is.

27. Revelation 17:11, And the *beast* that was, and is not, even he is the eighth, and is of the seven, and goeth into perdition.

28. Revelation 17:12, And the ten horns which thou sawest are ten kings, which have received no kingdom as yet; but receive power as kings one hour with the *beast*.

29. Revelation 17:13, These have one mind, and shall give their power and strength unto the *beast*.

30. Revelation 17:16, And the ten horns which thou sawest upon the *beast*, these shall hate the whore, and shall make her desolate and naked, and shall eat her flesh, and burn her with fire.

31. Revelation 17:17, For God hath put in their hearts to fulfil his will, and to agree, and give their kingdom unto the *beast*, until the words of God shall be fulfilled.

32. Revelation 19:19, And I saw the *beast*, and the kings of the earth, and their armies, gathered together to make war against him that sat on the horse, and against his army.

33. Revelation 19:20, And the *beast* was taken, and with him the false prophet that wrought miracles before him, with which he deceived them that had received the mark of the *beast*, and them that worshiped his image. These both were cast alive into a lake of fire burning with brimstone.

34. Revelation 20:4, And I saw thrones, and they sat upon them, and judgment was given unto them: and I saw the souls of them that were beheaded for the witness of Jesus, and for the word of God, and which had not worshiped the *beast*, neither his image, neither had received his mark upon their foreheads, or in their hands; and they lived and reigned with Christ a thousand years.

35. Revelation 20:10, And the devil that deceived them was cast into the lake of fire and brimstone, where the *beast*

and the false prophet are, and shall be tormented day and
night for ever and ever.

XXII. Necromancer or Charmer, 2 times

Deuteronomy 18:11, Or a *charmer*, or a consulter with
familiar spirits, or a wizard, or a *necromancer*.

XXIII. Wizards, 11 times

1. Leviticus 19:31, Regard not them that have familiar
spirits, neither seek after *wizards*, to be defiled by them: I am
the LORD your God.

2. Leviticus 20:6, And the soul that turneth after such
as have familiar spirits, and after *wizards*, to go a whoring
after them, I will even set my face against that soul, and will
cut him off from among his people.

3. Leviticus 20:27, A man also or woman that hath a
familiar spirit, or that is a *wizard*, shall surely be put to
death: they shall stone them with stones: their blood shall be
upon them.

4. Deuteronomy 18:11, Or a charmer, or a consulter
with familiar spirits, or a *wizard*, or a necromancer.

5. 1 Samuel 28:3, Now Samuel was dead, and all Israel
had lamented him, and buried him in Ramah, even in his own
city. And Saul had put away those that had familiar spirits,
and the *wizards*, out of the land.

6. 1 Samuel 28:9, And the woman said unto him,
Behold, thou knowest what Saul hath done, how he hath cut
off those that have familiar spirits, and the *wizards*, out of
the land: wherefore then layest thou a snare for my life, to
cause me to die?

7. 2 Kings 21:6, And he made his son pass through the
fire, and observed times, and used enchantments, and dealt
with familiar spirits and *wizards*: he wrought much

wickedness in the sight of the LORD, to provoke him to anger.

8. 2 Kings 23:24, Moreover the workers with familiar spirits, and the *wizards*, and the images, and the idols, and all the abominations that were spied in the land of Judah and in Jerusalem, did Josiah put away, that he might perform the words of the law which were written in the book that Hilkiah the priest found in the house of the LORD.

9. 2 Chronicles 33:6, And he caused his children to pass through the fire in the valley of the son of Hinnom: also he observed times, and used enchantments, and used witchcraft, and dealt with a familiar spirit, and with *wizards*: he wrought much evil in the sight of the LORD, to provoke him to anger.

10. Isaiah 8:19, And when they shall say unto you, Seek unto them that have familiar spirits, and unto *wizards* that peep, and that mutter: should not a people seek unto their God? for the living to the dead?

11. Isaiah 19:3, And the spirit of Egypt shall fail in the midst thereof; and I will destroy the counsel thereof: and they shall seek to the idols, and to the charmers, and to them that have familiar spirits, and to the *wizards*.

* * *

Notes . . .

Chapter **6**

Strategies for Exercising Authority

Churches and denominations today make several big mistakes. Probably you've noticed this.

They never teach about demons.

They do not minister deliverance to seekers.

They never teach how believers can gain the power and authority over the enemy.

There is so much that needs to be done—so many people who need help. Don't wait for the church or denomination to change their minds. You do it. Every believer should know how to exercise this authority.

If you're going into deliverance, three things are necessary: authority, discerning, and word of knowledge. All are supplied by the Holy Spirit. It could be a calling when the Spirit makes it of special interest to you. However in Mark 16, *"these signs shall follow those who believe."* Where are the believers? Some say not every one is called to that ministry, but is that true?

Casting out demons should be a standard part of church doctrine (Matthew 10:8), as is healing the sick. Healing and deliverance, it's in the same verse. It shouldn't be that church across town—all they do is cast out demons. It should be a standard part of ministry.

In our ministry, we have developed and redefined many new understandings because of questions people have asked. We would hold weekend mini-seminars to teach the concepts of *Don't Be Denied God's Power* and find out what concerns and problems the people were having.

What Is the basis for Our Authority?

I listed these verses in Chapter One, but to refresh your memory:

The Great Commission:

And Jesus came and spake unto them, saying, All power is given unto me in heaven and in earth. Go ye therefore, and teach all nations, baptizing them in the name of the Father, and of the Son, and of the Holy Ghost:

Teaching them to observe all things whatsoever I have commanded you: and, lo, I am with you alway, even unto the end of the world. Amen. (Matthew 28:18-20)

The Fivefold Commission:

1. *And as ye go, preach, saying, The kingdom of heaven is at hand.*

2. *Heal the sick,*

3. *cleanse the lepers,*

4. *raise the dead,*

5. *cast out devils:*

freely ye have received, freely give. (Matthew 10:7,8)

The Promise of the Holy Spirit:

But ye shall receive power, after that the Holy Ghost is come upon you: and ye shall be witnesses unto me both in Jerusalem, and in all Judaea, and in Samaria, and unto the uttermost part of the earth. (Acts 1:8)

What Helps? What hinders?

Do we get or improve or add to our authority by fasting? When Jesus' disciples could not cast out the demon in the child, He told them, *"This kind can come forth by nothing but prayer and fasting."* (Matthew 17:21; Mark 9:29) He didn't mean to start praying and fasting right then before ministering; this was something done in advance. Fasting breaks our flesh. In deliverance, our problem is to break their flesh so demons can get out. If you are serious about learning to minister deliverance you will want to consider learning how to fast.

Do we get or improve or add to our authority by doing anything? Authority, like muscle or faith, is made stronger by use.

Do we remove or diminish our authority by anything we do? Passivity takes a toll on our authority.

Does speaking in tongues help? If you mean praying in tongues—or unknown languages as it's sometimes referred to—this is not necessary; not mandatory. It may help. Once in a deliverance I did speak in an unknown language and the demon in the person said, "Don't talk that way. I don't know what you're saying."

In this chapter we'll take a look at some objections and then delve into four vital areas of concern.

Answering Objections

Many ministers object to the laying on of hands on the person being delivered, yet they believe in the laying on of hands for healing. Thirty years of experience has taught me that I can expel demons quicker by putting my hand where they are as I command them to leave, even though the pastors will tell you that Jesus never did this. I would rather do it this way, quickly, than have the spirits tear them as the Bible says. I have seen blood on the corner of a person's mouth and know that medical examinations prove that tearing takes place.

And as he was coming, the devil threw him down, and tore him. And Jesus rebuked the unclean spirit, and healed the child, and delivered him again to his father. (Luke 9:42)

Notice, too, that after Jesus rebuked (cast out) the demon, He had to heal the child.

I. Speak *Out Loud to* Your Delivered Self

People who read our last book, but who had no church where they could keep on learning about fighting off demons, revealed to us that although they had been delivered, they could not stay free from the harassing spirits. They would come back for more ministry, and be gloriously delivered again, but once they went home, they could not keep them out. We asked the Holy Spirit to teach us more.

We found we were not emphasizing enough how important it is for those believers to practice the biblical principles of speaking *out loud* to spirits which tried to re-enter them.

After we had delivered them with *out-loud* words, in the character and authority of Jesus, they would go home and be just wonderfully fine for a time, and then the demons would find a way to enter them again. *We had missed emphasizing that they needed to keep them out the same audible way we had gotten them out in the first place.*

The more we worked with them, the more we learned to teach them that they needed to *quickly* tell the demons (of fear or jealousy or depression or anger) to mind their own business. We are all tempted to relax and fall prone to not handling everyday problems with verbal words empowered by His authority. If they had been aware of, and spoken to, these demons out loud in the first place they never would have been able to come in *except during trauma where they had no control over the initial situation.*

Now they needed to acquire these skills of speaking to the temptations out loud, as I had at their initial deliverance, while the harassing demons were still outside of their bodies. *"The fiery darts of the wicked"* (Ephesians 6:16) will come and try to convince you to do what is stupid, but you *don't* have to listen, and you *do* have to talk back. Like Jesus in the wilderness (Matthew 4), you don't have to conversations or argue with them. Just speak a few authoritative words, and go on with your godly walk with Christ Jesus.

When they learned to do this, they were amazed to find out that the demons they feared were no longer able to enter them again. "Leave me alone," or, "Go, I am not yours, I belong to Jesus," or, "I am the Lord's and will listen to Him alone!" are a few good examples of great ways to obey the commandment to *"Resist the devil"* (any one that comes along, big or little) *"and he will flee from you."* (James 4:7) They really do flee, because they know they have to! They will want to con you into believing they're not there. But they are and they will go when they see you know it.

It was great to get those phone calls and letters where overcomers would tell us of these new victories. We have saved much of this correspondence and rejoice over them.

Carol had suffered since her teen years from a very religious spirit that told her that she was ugly without make-up, and she was purposely sensual to attract men if she wore *any* at all. She had come from a denomination that abhorred women wearing make-up. She was delivered, but had a great deal of religious condemnation (from those same demons who called her wicked if she did, and wicked if she didn't!).

Finally, the Holy Spirit showed me the answer. I told her to tell those demons (which were outside of her, not on the inside) that, "It's *none* of your business. This is between God and me. Now bug off." This worked beautifully. After a few days they got sick and tired of being told it was none of their business and left her alone.

I began using this strategy myself when I made mistakes and condemnation came upon me for messing up, both in my personal life and in ministering to others. It still works today. God is so good to show us better ways of handling each new situation with the same principles of rebuking the enemy that were there all along. Jesus said, *"Get thee behind me."* The new generation says, "Bug off!" It's still the authority behind the Words coming from the Spirit who abides within us that gets it done!

Many of the critically demonized folks could have kept the demons from entering them, long before it got to the critical stage, if the church had just taught them to speak out loud to the demons that were harassing them just slightly in the beginning, but had not yet entered them.

Josie, a single, divorced mom, came to us because her six and eight year-old boys were displaying strange, irrational, hateful, and violent behaviors. (They really enjoyed hurting people and animals.) The Holy Spirit taught us a good spiritual lesson we will never forget.

I had initially delivered them from some demons and there had been immediate improvement which had continued for weeks. But the boys had to leave her home and live with their very sinful father every couple of weekends and their behavior was always terrible when they returned.

She called us on one such occasion when her son, Jason, was being totally uncontrollable. She feared that his behavior would allow the demons to enter him again. We suggested that she go and wrap her arms around him tightly and say, with all the authority in Christ that had been given to her, "You demons leave my son alone! He's *my* son. I love him, he loves Jesus, he's a good boy and he doesn't belong to you, he belongs to *me*. So be gone!"

She did it immediately and called us within the hour to tell us of the wonderful change that happened to him. He had calmed down and started playing with his toys again as normal as could be.

A couple of days later she heard him hollering in his room, and fearing that he was going off the deep end again, she raced down the hall to him. She stopped at the doorway just in time to hear him say, "You demons, you leave me alone. I'm not going to do that because I'm a good boy, God loves me, and my Mommy loves me and I belong to her, not you . . . so be gone!" Then he happily began to play by himself again.

We realized that if children are taught this before they go off the deep end, there would be much more authority over demons on a daily basis. If we just had that childlike nature to accept the teachings of Jesus before we become so entrenched with doubt, we would be a much more wise and powerful church.

Check Your Home's Décor

A further point of information we've learned. Check your house for demons, and clean it. Or have somebody do it for you who can discern spirits. Some objects may be questionable; however, I urge you to rid your home of such things as idols brought home by tourists, wind chimes, and anything relating to satanic objects. Frogs and owls are especially dangerous.

II. Demons in the Head vs. Demons in the Rest of the Body

We also learned more about the difference between demons in the head and demons in the rest of the body. Ones which came out of the head manifested differently from those cast out of the bodies.

Demons in the arms and legs can often be felt by the person. They could feel them move around inside, or move out as I spoke to them. Demons in the abdomen or body cavity would often come out the mouth causing such conditions as coughing, choking, yawning, retching, grunting, whining, screaming, or the like. We can rebuke and silence the demons and they will not act out as strongly.

Those which came out of the head seemed to make no noise nor be felt in such obvious ways. Janice, our publisher's computer analyst, did say she sensed something like an egg in her head that cracked and then oozed down the inside of her brain, coming out both ears.

But *mostly* they showed none of these signs.

We asked many of them how they felt after demons had been cast out of their head, and most said they "felt it was lighter," or "less heavy," or "like a pressure has been released," or "more relaxed." Many times they said it felt like a band around the head on the outside, and left when they were delivered. We realized that these answers showed a common phenomena: that the demons had somehow taken up room in the brain, and that once they were removed there was an emptying of that particular space.

Sometimes we would ask them to describe how they felt, and they couldn't quite tell us. Then I would say something like, "Could you describe it perhaps like a football that had been released of a little of its air?" and inevitably a smile of recognition would cross their face, and they would say, "Yeah! That's it!"

Demons in the head were often responsible for much depression and manic depressive behaviors. After deliverance, many believers with mental illnesses slowly came off of their medications when they and their doctors saw how much better they were able to handle life. Many said something like, "Is *this* what a normal head feels like?!" It was a real surprise to them. We never told any of them to go off their medications.

The Holy Spirit revealed the truth to me of demons being in the head. Most teachers of deliverance have not known about demons in the head. They may do deliverance of demons in the body but miss those in the head.

III. Particular Demonic Manifestations in Women

Many women now feel able to talk about sexual problems. This is how we learned about what Webster's Dictionary calls "incubus." They are spirits that attack women (mostly in the night) in their sexual organs and cause them to react sexually, just as if they were having intercourse with a man. I believe that it is happening to more women now because of the acceptance and flaunting of sexual perversions. Books, videos, media, TV programming, music and the like, target women for this demonic experience.

A similar occurrence in men is "succubus." No doubt this is also a problem, but we are not aware of this affecting many men. The principles for deliverance are the same, however.

Incubus demons have been around for a long time. We saw them years ago in those who came for deliverance, but they are much more common now. These spirits are assigned to women who are weak in this area, who have had a history of sexual abuse or promiscuity, who have a great deal of unbiblical confusion about sexual issues, or who are not getting the sexual fulfillment God intended them to have in their marriages.

Women can be easily delivered once they understand what is going on. They generally come to us scared and embarrassed that they have such a problem, but have heard that their problem might be evil spirits and that we know how to deal with such matters.

We always ask women with this problem to bring a woman friend or her husband (or both) when she comes to talk about it or be delivered. My wife, or another godly woman who has experience in ministry to women with this problem, is also always present. We have the woman seeking deliverance place her hand over her ovaries or sexual organs and I command the demons to come out. They can practically always feel them leave. Then, before they go home we pray for their spiritual strength so they'll not let the demons return to try and harass them from the outside. We teach them to do spiritual warfare to fight off these spirits. This is the procedure we teach.

1. *The instant you are aware of a demon, get up and change your position physically.* If you are in bed, move to a chair in the living room or kitchen. You must show them that you, not them, have authority over what your body does. This is just a first step, but it is very important because they still want you. Get up. Get moving. Get in control of your own body.

2.) *Tell the demon to leave immediately.*

3. *Ask God to intervene.* If you are born again, thank Him for the blood-covenant that you have with God. Remember that you belong to Him alone because of that gift of the blood that Jesus gave to buy you back to Himself.

If you feel like you have done something to blatantly let the spirit come back to tempt you (like watching a pornographic movie or soap opera, or if you entertained impure sexual thoughts on purpose), then wholeheartedly ask God for forgiveness.

Caution: If you enjoy this relationship, if you nurture it and play with it, if you "toy" with it in any way, it can be an open door for other spirits to begin to enter your flesh as well, and you will become tormented by the very thing that you find "fascinating" as it comes to "flirt" with you.

After this repentance is clearly done in your heart, then thank Him that His Word is true, that when you confess your sins He is faithful and just to forgive you your sins and that you are now cleansed from it again. (1 John 1:9)

Don't let any condemnation from the enemy try to convince you that this was all your fault and that you really want him to stay. Remember: "*There is, therefore, now* **no** *condemnation to them who are in Christ.*" (Romans 8:1,emphasis added) Say this out loud because it is true, and your ears need to hear your mouth say so, because this is a common tactic of the enemy to get you to stop fighting. He likes to make you take the blame for what *he's* doing to you! Don't fall for it. He's the dummy and you're the one with Christ Jesus in you.

Keep moving forward in this battle. Tell this evil spirit that you are laying down the law because the next verse says that "*the law of the Spirit of life in Christ Jesus hath made me* **free** *from the law of sin and death.*" (verse 2, emphasis added) You are the overcomer. Say it!

4. *Turn on the enemy wholeheartedly.* Pick up your Sword, which is the Word of God. Get out your Bible and hold it up and claim that God, Himself, the Author of *this* Book is your Husband and your Authority. Declare to the enemy that you will not let any other spirit being touch you. Remind him that he is a defeated foe, and that he may not trespass on territory that belongs to Christ Jesus.

Command him to leave. He will. He hates to be told he is unwanted. The evil spirit is like a boyfriend who keeps coming over, even though you've told him you're not interested any more. He feels rejected. Keep him getting the message. Remember this is your job. You may have to do it for several days, or even longer.

Read those scriptures again so that the authority you have been given will rise up in you, and your faith in God's Word about who you really are (instead of what your emotions say) will rule here. This is your God-given *job*. The victory was made to be *yours*. Use your mouth to release the words of the Spirit of God within you, and your authority in Him will rebuke the enemy again and again. *Stand* against him consistently and that battle will be won. *"Take unto you the whole armor of God, that you may be able to with*stand *in the evil day, and having done all, to* **stand**.*"* (Ephesians 6:13, emphasis added)

After you get the victory over this one, tell your friends! You have no idea how this testimony needs to be heard by women who are keeping this thing a secret, in the darkness where they think they are the only one experiencing it. When women know there are real answers in the Word, this will bring them out of the dark closet and into the healing light of God through you. This authority is to be shared with a scared and hurting world where demons have had much too much freedom to hurt the beautiful Bride of Christ!

This good news will also bring many unbelievers to see that what they think is "the prudish world of pie-in-the-sky Christianity" is nothing of the sort, but is where reality begins and can be faced with real answers.

IV. "Priming the Pump"

Deliverance used to take me a long time . . . anywhere from half an hour to several hours, until the

Lord showed me a strategy and a Biblical principle that made the demons obey faster and leave sooner. I saw people asking for deliverance, and then, during deliverance, their flesh didn't want to let go. They would sometimes cover their mouth with their hand as if trying not to let the demons out. Or they would tighten their lips together.

Abby, a young person who came for deliverance, stuck the side of her finger in her mouth and bit down. Her flesh was trying to keep the demon in, but her eyes pleaded with me to get it out. She was in obvious pain from biting the side of her finger.

I asked the Holy Spirit why people did this, and it occurred to me that it wasn't the demons that were holding onto the person, but it was the person's flesh not wanting to let go, even though the spirit of the person wanted them out. So, to get the person's flesh in agreement with me, I would ask them to cough to get their body to agree with us that it was to let go. They would cough a couple of times on purpose, and then would begin to cough out of control as the demons came out.

I call this "priming the pump" because although the first few coughs are self-imposed, the coughing that follows expel the demons. This process made deliverance happen much sooner. I looked back and saw that much of the time I had spent trying to cast out the demons had *really* been spent fighting the person's flesh to let go.

This is another example of the "principle of agreement."

> *Verily I say unto you, Whatsoever ye shall bind on earth shall be bound in heaven: and whatsoever ye shall loose on earth shall be loosed in heaven. Again I say unto you, That if two of you shall agree on earth as touching any thing that they shall ask, it shall be done for them by my Father who is in heaven.* (Matthew 18:18,19)

Agreeing with God that these folks seeking deliverance shall be loosed from the demons, and then getting them to get their own bodies to agree that they *will* to be loosed of the demons is a powerful agreement factor.

I believe that when one person agrees with the Word, that includes agreement with Father, Son, and Holy Spirit. Right there you have more than two in agreement. If other people agree, too, that's all the more in agreement.

I am even more impressed that the next verse re-emphasizes that it is the *name* of Jesus, His character and authority reproduced in His obedient children, those willing to be like Him, to whom these promises are made. *"For where two or three are gathered together in my name, there am I in the midst of them."* (Matthew 18:20) Can you see this familiar verse in the new light you now have about His *name?*

God's answers were always there, in the Word, only we had missed some things that were right under our noses. Haven't you wondered at the things that are hidden at first, and yet in plain sight?

The Power of the Tongue

The words we speak reveal to everyone who hears them the condition of our heart. *"Out of the abundance of the heart the mouth speaketh."* (Matthew 12:34; Luke 6:45)

If our heart is full of the Holy Spirit and we love the Lord, it will be evident by our speech. This is a serious matter. We are to speak the power and authority of Jesus Christ into all situations. But we can also talk ourselves out of power and authority. We can talk ourselves out of healing and good health. Are you guilty of uttering such foolishness?

"My shoulder is killing me."

"I'm sick and tired of . . . "

"That just burns me up."

"What's the use?"

"I'm just dying to . . . "

"Whatever will be, will be."

"That situation is driving me crazy."

"Poor old me."

Banish faithless words. Fill your heart and your mouth with powerful words. We can even command God! *"Thus saith the LORD, the Holy One of Israel, and his Maker, Ask me of things to come concerning my sons, and concerning the work of my hands command ye me."* (Isaiah 45:11) Obviously, we must be in agreement with God to be able to take such a strong position.

We must know the Word. We *must* know the Word. We must know the *Word*. And, above all, we must know *Him*.

* * *

More of Stan's sayings...

You can have Jesus *now* as your Savior,
Healer, and Friend or you will have Him *later*
. . . as your Judge.

If it's a spiritual problem you'd better deal
with it, or it will deal with you.

Faith does not add.
If I can climb only halfway up the mountain
and you can climb only halfway up the
mountain, we will not make it to the top.
My half of faith will not add to
your half of faith.

When God says to do it,
do it before you have time to work up doubt.

It's not the giants,
nor seeing the giants;
it's our perception of the giants
that leads to fear and failure.

God is never late.

Chapter **7**

Authority Over
Curses and Demons

Curses are real. Demons are real. This should not make us fearful; it should make us bold enough to use the authority God gives us to evict these unwanted intruders.

I've been cursed; no doubt, you have too.

The Truth About Curses

Words sent to do damage against Christians are actual curses. Curses can powerfully influence us in the spirit realm. For it to be a curse there doesn't have to be any actual ritual or the spoken words "curse" or "damn." Demons will use people, even jealous and unschooled, immature Christians to say terrible things against other believers and Christian ministries.

Two types of curses are most commonly known. One is family curses from our ancestors or our parents which cause personality traits in us that we have to overcome. Another is the kind of curse that keeps us emotionally bound to someone, against God's counsel not to be unequally yoked (2 Corinthians 6:14) with those who are spiritually the opposite of us—for example, living together without being married, or being part of an ungodly business contract. This is sometimes called a "soul tie."

Where there has been sexual relations, the two have become "one flesh" (1 Corinthians 6:16). In this situation, the sin needs to be confessed and the soul ties need to be renounced.

We can rebuke and cut off these kinds of curses. We just need to be aware of them and boldly command them to be of no effect to us anymore.

The James Curses

We've not generally been aware of the kind of curse I call the "James curse." It is a curse sent by a Christian.

James talks about words which come out of our mouths that cause both blessing or cursing. *"Out of the same mouth proceed blessing and cursing. My brethren, these things ought not so to be."* (James 3:10) Interesting that he is talking about the mouths of our brethren! It is brethren—other Christians—that have the spiritual power to both bless and curse us! It was amazing for me to discover that we can use this power that resides in every believer against each other.

We must be so careful to wield this power against the enemy *only*, as James is warning us about here. We have learned how to get rid of these curses by identifying them through a word of knowledge, canceling the curse, and commanding the effects of them to no longer hurt us.

Marilyn was a lady who came to me to be healed. She had been cursed, but did not know it. Over a period of nine years, she gradually was overcome with depression and fatigue so severely that her hair began falling out and her teeth were loosening. God showed me by a word of knowledge that a curse had been put upon her. Her husband and she both immediately affirmed that there was a Christian woman who had done this. We took authority over the curse and sent it back to where they had come from. There was an immediate response in Marilyn's soul and spirit.

Later as she was working in her kitchen, something happened where she spontaneously said, "Praise the Lord!" She told us she had not been able to say those words for years without struggling to get them out. From that moment on her healing started, and she continued to get better and better again in her walk with the Lord.

Are We to Send These Curses Back?

Recently, I personally experienced the effects of a curse on me. I found myself getting exhausted for absolutely no reason and getting grouchy at people around me, even though they had done nothing to make me react like that. I asked the Spirit to show me what was happening.

He showed me that people who were offended by my ministry were being used of the devils to curse me. One woman in particular, "Laura", was telling the ladies in her home Bible study that she knew my ministry would fail because I had married the wrong woman after I had been widowed.

In retrospect, I wish I had handled this revelation from the Holy Spirit more maturely, but I have to confess that I was furious with her and I promptly sent the curse back to *her*, and relished what might happen to her! Forgive me, but that's what I did. However, the effects of the curses stopped harassing me when I did this. So I figured I had found the key to this kind of spiritual warfare against curses.

One day not long afterwards, I learned that she had slipped on her wet kitchen floor and fell, hitting the socket of her left eye on the corner of the refrigerator door. Her face was horribly blackened and she began having headaches.

I wondered if this wasn't the result of the returned curses, and began to feel very guilty that my strategy was really giving license to the devils to harm her. And worse, the old exhaustion and anger at people around me began to return.

It was then I was reminded by the Holy Spirit that I had actually been cursing another believer by sending back those demons! This was a new revelation to me. My emotions had gotten in the way of realizing that we are *not* to curse them that curse us.

The Holy Spirit showed me that I was to send the curse back *to the devils* who were suggesting to her that she speak these jealous words against me. I silenced the demons *behind* the person who was sending the words. In this way I got rid of them, and could be used of God to help her stop being used by the enemy to hurt us both. It worked much better than the temporary solution I had used before. What a lesson.

I wished that I had remembered sooner that we cannot return curses to hurt the person who was used of the devil to hurt us. *"Bless them that curse you."* (Matthew 5:44; Luke 6:28) *"Bless them who persecute you; bless and curse not."* (Romans 12:14)

Our motive and our attitude towards the person is to bless them. This is where the enemy would love to divide and conquer the believers, so we will not stand together against him. He would love to make it seem "only reasonable and fair" to hurt the Christian brother or sister doing this against you, causing havoc in their lives and keeping them from the best that the kingdom of God has to offer. But we have become mindful of his schemes and will not use the devil's tactics to fight him back. God's great tactics are a thousand times better.

James 3:9 says, *"The tongue can no man tame; it is an unruly evil, full of deadly poison."* So without God, man cannot tame his own tongue. However, the good news is that with God the tongue can be tamed to bless and not curse.

Take Care of These Curses Daily

If you find yourself suddenly feeling exhausted for no apparent reason, or feel extreme depression, these are two obvious clues that you have been cursed by someone.

As part of our evening devotions we routinely send back any curses that have been sent against us during that day. We specifically say that *we send the curse back to the demonic spirit behind the person who said the words.* We rebuke that demon, tell it to be silent and not to communicate any more with that person. We tell the demon it has to leave immediately and not return.

Protection from Demons That Follow You Home

I was never afraid of getting demons into myself by delivering people from demons. But I did find that they would follow me home and influence my family life if I did not command them not to. It was easy to do this when I remembered, but sometimes I forgot out of negligence or laziness.

The trauma of the death of Susie, a beloved family dog, taught me the next lesson. I allowed myself to grieve much too long after her death. Missing her terribly and nursing my emotional wounds, I found myself in a deep state of grief that I could not escape. In that condition, not being in control of my flesh, the demon that followed me home after a deliverance session in Colorado found easy access into my head. I became aware of its presence because it felt like a golf ball rolling back and forth from one side of my head to the other. Realizing what it was, I had my wife command it to leave and it did instantly. Then I commanded it out of my house, never to return. This incident helped me to remember more often to not let them follow me home.

The Cause of Nightmares

The Holy Spirit taught me another good lesson on how to get rid of nightmares. I had once thought they were just a part of ordinary life where dreams and thoughts in the night scare you into physically reacting to the stresses of everyday living. But He showed me that I was having dreadful dreams about snakes before I was to deliver a person the next day. I found that demons were just trying to scare me ahead of time.

I have allowed demons to come home with me from hospitals. Demons have to leave when people die and in the hospital they looked for other people who were traumatized, expecting to gain entrance. They followed me home, hoping that I would make some mistake to open the door. They could not enter, but would torment me with thoughts that influenced my dreams. After I got up and commanded them to leave, I could sleep peacefully.

I used this new knowledge and strategy to teach parents about keeping their homes clean of demons if they had to go to hospitals and brought home demons that plagued their children. This strategy worked for them also again and again.

Angie called me about her children who were having constant nightmares. Looking for the source of this harassment, I was led to ask her where her husband worked. She said he was an inspector for the State Hospital Board. I recognized the problem and told her it couldn't be a better set-up for the devils to be following him home. She believed me, but didn't know if her husband would accept it. She called her mother, who was also a strong believer in the Word of God, and they agreed together that Al, her husband, would listen to them with open ears and then have some kind of experience that would cause him to believe this principle. He listened attentively, but really wasn't that enthusiastic.

One day soon afterwards, he came out of a hospital and got into his van. Then he remembered to command the demons out of his van, and did so. Immediately, the window behind his left ear exploded outward as the demons exited at his command. It made a real believer of him, and he has kept his house clean of demons ever since. And, of course, nightmares no longer victimize his children.

Here's another example. Once when I came home from a deliverance session, I didn't realize that demons had followed me. They found opportunity to enter my wife. After a few days I realized what was going on and I commanded them to leave. A demon spoke and said, "Oh, I thought you liked us."

"Where did you get that idea?"

"You let us follow you home."

" From where?"

"You know, from that house on the other side of town."

"Well, you can't stay. Get out."

God Wants Us to Learn About This

From these and other experiences I was aware that demons can talk out loud. I knew better than to engage them in any long conversations.

Not everything is the fault of demons. It is ridiculous to blame them and look for them everywhere, because most things are not caused by demons. But on the other hand, if we do not find them where they *are*, and learn to rebuke and cast them out, we are going to be harassed by them when they do find access into our lives.

We must be responsible to recognize where they are and where they aren't. It's like learning the difference between what works in trying to clean up certain messes. Trying to clean up after oil-based paint job with a strong soap and some water just makes a bigger mess. Use some paint thinner, and the job is done in a hurry. Alternately, paint thinner is not going to work on a water-based paint job, but soap and water works immediately.

Be smart and find the biblical answers, not the world-based ones. Don't let anyone do your homework for you. Paul says, *"The Word is nigh thee even in thy mouth."* (Romans 10:8) We have no excuse, even if we didn't "hear it right" from our pastor or church. The truth is closer than our church or our pastor. We could be on a desert island with our Bible and His Spirit and we could still get it right.

Take Care of These Intruders Daily

If you have been somewhere during the day where demonic spirits are likely to be present, evict these intruders at that time, or at least by bedtime. Such spirits as fear, anger, depression, and confusion would likely be in hospitals, doctors' offices, dentists' offices, etc. Remember, these spirits are everywhere, looking for a place to enter. They can follow you home, hoping to find an entrance into you or your children.

As part of our evening devotions, we routinely cast out any spirits that have followed us home. We tell the demon it has to leave immediately and is not allowed to return. Then we ask the Lord to give us a restful night so we will be not troubled by foolish dreams, and so we can awaken with bodies restored and ready for the new day.

We Have the Authority Over Them

In Matthew 4:1-11, where Jesus was led by the Spirit into the desert to be tempted by the devil, He quoted Scripture to refute him. (verses 4,7,10). When Jesus commanded, "Get thee hence, Satan," then Satan left Him. Two other Gospel writers also give an account of this temptation (Mark 1:13; Luke 4:1-13). Luke's account notes in verse 13 that *"when the devil had ended all the temptation, he departed from him for a season."* It goes on to say in verse 14, *"And Jesus returned in the power of the Spirit into Galilee: and there went out a fame of him through all the region round about."*

This tells us that it is no sin to be tempted. We can rebuke the devil on the authority of the Scripture, and after each victorious encounter, we can go out to minister successfully by the power of the Holy Spirit.

Later in His years of ministry, as Jesus cast out demons from people who came to Him, we note that He did not enter into a lengthy dialogue with these spirits. In a few words He commanded them to come out and leave. And He always won.

We will be tested and tried. God allows this for our learning and strengthening.

Yes, curses and demons are real. They can trouble us, harass us, and, given the opportunity, they can get into us. It's part of our responsibility as growing Christians to take care of these pesky enemies.

There's a Time to *Pray*, and There's a Time to *Say*

God has so much more for us, if we'll only take hold of it. We must learn when to pray about it and when to rise up with His authority and *say it.*

> *Whosoever shall say unto this mountain, Be thou removed, and be thou cast into the sea; and shall not doubt in his heart, but shall believe that those things which he saith shall come to pass, he shall have whatever he saith.* (Mark 11:23)

God has commanded us to use the authority He's given us.

* * *

Chapter **8**

Authority to Judge?

What's keeping you from obeying what God has told you to do?

Embarrassment?

Fear of attracting the attention of Satan, and becoming his target?

Unwillingness to break free from a pattern of confusion?

Unwillingness to let go of some secret sin?

Is it apathy? Passivity? Neglect?

The biggest thing is probably church doctrine.

We've probably not given much thought to the reality of sin. To sin intentionally is rebellion against God.

All around us we see Christians who appear to be apathetic or passive. They seem to be content to just occupy the pew on Sunday and try to be upstanding citizens for the rest of the week. Did Jesus call us to be "good"?

Whose problem is it if I am not growing into maturity and boldness and obedience to God? Is maturity an automatic process that just happens? Can I just rest on Jesus, claim the promises, and hold on?

No, dear believers. God has a mighty work for you and me to do. And, instead of reclining on clouds in the sky in the sweet-by-and-by, playing on harps, and everlastingly singing to Him, there are responsibilities we must concern ourselves with right now. We are to reign with Him in the millennium here on earth.

There's Work to Do

We must keep asking ourselves, "What is *my* part, and what is *God's* part in making me ready for this upcoming millennium reign with Him?"

Look ahead to see what John saw in his vision. Listen to the voice of the multitude:

> *Let us be glad and rejoice, and give honor to him; for the marriage of the Lamb is come, and his wife hath made herself ready. And to her was granted that she should be arrayed in fine linen, clean and white; for the fine linen is the righteousness of saints.* (Revelation 19:7,8)

By this time the Bride has been *prepared*. There is no time in heaven for her to work on herself. She has already been in training somewhere else to be a good wife. Jesus has made her clean with His blood so that she is righteous in His sight by what He did for her on the cross, but something else has happened here. "She" is those who have already overcome the enemy on earth. She is *not* just a sweet and innocent, gentle little nobody.

In obedience to Him, here on earth, as His Betrothed Beloved one, she had learned to victoriously wield the Sword of the Spirit, wearing the armor of God to fight His enemy, and rule over the hordes of the enemy in His name. She, the Church, did not just thank Him for saving her so she could then lay down and take whatever Satan assigned against her.

If I am being readied to reign with Him, I need to know how to lead. We know that to be a good leader, we must first be a good follower. We know that first we must be a servant to those we minister to, as Jesus said, *And whosoever of you will be the chiefest, shall be servant of all. For even the Son of man came, not to be ministered unto, but to minister, and to give his life a ransom for many.* (Mark 10:44,45)

2 Timothy 2:12—*"If we suffer, we shall also reign with Him"* (emphasis added) (# 4821)

Revelation 20:6—". . . *shall reign* with *him a thousand years.* " (emphasis added)

Getting Out on the Limb

When we teach about the authority and character of God *in* us to overcome the world, too many people think, at first, that we have to muster up the strength to obey God and go ahead to fight the enemy with human resolve and determination.

On the other hand, there are those who think that if they can isolate themselves and just stay in the Word, God will do everything for them without them *getting up* and using their energy *to go* to where the action is with others—whether it's downtown, on a mission field, or in a church.

The truth is that the work of God to perfect the saints is worked out together, both spiritually and emotionally with other imperfect (but being perfected!) soldiers of God. We get out on the limb together. We fight in the foxholes together.

God's ministry to us, as He perfects us, always includes making us work with others, like iron sharpens iron, to fight off our enemies together. We must learn to judge others and they must learn to judge us. In order to do this we must first judge ourselves.

"Judge Not"?

Many people quote the scripture "judge not" when a criticism comes their way, in order to keep others from correcting them. They fail to look at the rest of that chapter where God goes on to explain *how* to judge correctly, in the spirit and not in the flesh.

There are two words in the Bible translated into "judge" in English. One is in Matthew 7:1, *"judge not that ye be not judged."* (Strong's #2919 *krino* means to determine, condemn, go to law, pronounce opinion.)

The second is in 1 Corinthians 6:5, *" I speak to your shame. Is it so, that there is not a wise man among you? No, not one that shall be able to judge between his brethren? "* (Strong's #350 *anakrino* means to examine, investigate, scrutinize, interrogate, determine.)

We see that *if* we learn to judge ourselves correctly, *then* we *will* be able to judge others.

There are definitely splinters in other people's eyes, but the splinter in our own eyes is like a plank that keeps us from ourselves—and them—in the Spirit as God sees. Our plank is our huge human weakness that makes us blind as to how much we need the gifts and fruit of the Spirit. Before we pronounce a verdict about others, we must first learn to judge ourselves.

Jesus Tells Us to Judge

Jesus tells us to *"beware of false prophets, who come to you in sheep's clothing, but inwardly they are ravening wolves."* (Matthew 7:15) How will you know this without judging them to be false?

"Wherefore by their fruits ye shall know them." (Matthew 7:20) How can you tell if their fruits are good if you can't judge?

Paul Knew How to Judge

Paul knew about judging correctly when he told the Philippians that he prayed *"that your love may abound yet more and more in knowledge and in all judgment; that you may approve things that are excellent"* (Philippians 1:9-11) "Approve" (#1381 *dok-i-ma-zo*) means to discern, examine, test. Does that sound like they are not to judge?

Then Paul goes on to instruct them to judge those in their midst who preach Christ *"out of envy and strife,"* and those who are preaching *"of good will."* (verse 15)

He also teaches the Corinthian believers that *"the natural man receiveth not the things of the Spirit of God; for they are foolishness unto him, neither can he know them, because they are spiritually discerned. But he that is spiritual judgeth all things, yet he himself is judged of no man"* (1 Corinthians 2:14,15)

Paul says, *"Do you not judge them that are within?"* (1 Corinthians 5:12). He is concerned that they are not putting out of their church the fornication among them and the one who is having his father's wife (1 Corinthians 5:1-12). If we are not willing to be taught how to judge in love, then we will foolishly let sin ruin our churches.

Further, Paul declares, *"Know ye not that we shall judge angels? How much more things that pertain to this life?"* (1 Corinthians 6:3) For him, teaching the believers how to judge is a serious matter.

How Does This Apply to Us?

We should not judge others by the natural inclinations or a hard-hearted attitude, but we must learn to judge by the Spirit of God who lives within us. He requires us to hear Him and speak His words to others.

Don't let men pronounce judgment upon you, but do let God use a man to judge you and your fruit, so that both he and you can grow together to have the *"mind of Christ."* (1 Corinthians 2:16)

Our motive in judging is our love of one another and our desire to see each other grow up in the Spirit. Then we can catch the enemy at his tricks and cast him down. We can judge a person as wonderfully righteous and point out his gifts to him. Or, by the same Spirit, we can encourage him to stop doing what is keeping him from becoming an overcomer.

Make yourself available, with no strings attached, to be both judged and to be matured into someone who can be used of God to judge the Bride of Christ with righteous judgment. Give Him permission to use His gifts in you.

Learning how to judge righteously is one of the major ways we make ourselves ready to be the Bride. He will teach us how, but we are to do it.

God says that our efforts must be *"not by might nor by power, but by My Spirit."* (Zechariah 4:6) ("Might" here, #2428, is *chayil*, and means human force, an army.) This does not mean that He does it by Himself. We do it in His character and authority. This is our part and our responsibility in the Covenant. To be an overcomer is not just to claim a title and a reward. It means we've been in the battle, we've followed our Commander, and we've gained the victory.

Yes, Satan and his demons will be defeated in the end. God is in control. The outcome is never in doubt.

The Principle of Agreement Is Underscored

When we do what God tells us to do, we are coming into agreement with Him. (Would we really want to disagree or argue with God?) We're in a Covenant relationship with God, and in a covenant there are always two parties who must agree to one written clause. We are to allow the Holy Spirit to teach our spirit, and our soul is to be renewed with the Word. When we come into agreement with God, we have His power and His authority. It's that simple; and it is that profound.

Does the Devil Go to Your Church?

I think we're sadly mistaken if we think that entering the local church building makes us immune from demonic influence. Ask yourself, Where can the devils do the most damage? Look at what the devils do in church:

water down the truth of God's Word,

stir up dissension,

mix in false doctrine,

wear us out with busy work,

pit us against each other to stimulate pride,

skim off money which should go to winning souls,

dazzle us with show-off projects,

set up competition between your church and the other churches,

point out the faults of everyone so you can feel superior,

delegate all the power gifts and ministry to the clergy,

confuse us with too many versions of the Bible,

give us an arena for hurt feelings.

I've seen people in churches fuss over the color of the new carpeting. I've seen people take offense at what Sister Jones brought for the church supper. There have been splits over the budget and over the Sunday school curriculum. The pastor smiles too much and it reminds us of a used car salesman. The pastor doesn't smile enough and it reminds us of the IRS agent downtown.

Is this what happens on Sunday morning at your church?

We sing, "I Surrender All," but are too busy to go to the midweek service.

We sing, "What a Friend We Have in Jesus," but only speak to Him in church.

We sing, "onward, Christian Soldiers," but our church has not taught us about the enemy or how to win in the everyday battle.

We sing, "Nearer, My God, to Thee," and haven't gotten around to getting any closer to Him.

Words flow so glibly from our mouths. Do we mean what we say? Do we agree with what God says?

When will we learn to look at these things God's way? When will we come into agreement with His written Word and the Holy Spirit within us?

> *But strong meat belongeth to them that are of full age, even those who by reason of use have their senses exercised to discern both good and evil.* (Hebrews 5:14)

God does not judge our success by the evidence and outcomes we see, but by our obedience that He sees. Come on, people, you can do it.

* * *

Chapter **9**

Our Authority—
In the Spotlight

You get authority by taking it and using it. A police uniform and badge don't do anything until the officer puts them on. They don't do anything unless he or she is authorized by a higher power to use them. They don't do anything unless he or she gets out and confronts the trouble.

God Himself has authorized us to use His power and authority. He's given us what we need. He's spoken to us, each one of us, personally. Perhaps we haven't heard His quiet voice in His Word, or in the quiet hours of private devotion and prayer. But He has spoken to us, to me and to you.

The sooner we stop acting double-minded, the sooner we can get on with being the bold believers, the overcomers.

We've been taught to think we can't. Now you know. We *can*.

Since God is no respecter of persons, Peter couldn't have had more power and authority than we do. Paul and the other disciples couldn't have had more power and authority than we do. Circumstances may be different, but the principles are the same.

The Greatest Love Story in the Bible

God in His wonderful love has given us gifts that we've not even thought about very much. Read a wonderful love story in Genesis 24.

Father Abraham wants to get a suitable bride for his son, Isaac, so he sends his faithful servant Eliezar to his home country, with ten camels laden with gifts. When the servant gets near the city, he prays that God will send the chosen girl out to him, and that she will have a servant's heart, willing to give him a drink of water and also water the camels. As he is speaking, a beautiful girl comes up and does just that. Then the servant gives her several gifts. After the girl tells her family that she is willing to leave right away for the trip back to marry Isaac, the servant brings out many more precious gifts. Shortly, Rebekah, the beautiful bride-to-be, is on a camel, traveling with the servant, on that long trip back to the waiting groom.

This depicts for us how Father God has sent His Holy Spirit, laden with gifts, to find us, the prospective Bride of Christ. The Holy Spirit gives us the gifts. Obviously, we must be willing to receive and take them.

We must be willing to start out at once on the journey towards our new home, where the Father and the Son are waiting. As we travel, we have the wonderful companionship of the Holy Spirit. We can converse with Him, ask Him questions, learn from Him. He never leaves us, but accompanies us all the way.

Remember this on your own personal journey to *home*. The Holy Spirit is there with you, and He wants to be your best friend. Talk to Him all day long. There is no jealousy or separation or difference of motives or power between God the Father, God the Son, and God the Holy Spirit. When we accept Jesus as Savior, we are pledging ourselves to Him, to be His forever in a relationship that the Bible describes as Bride to Bridegroom. What love.

Seeing this deeper meaning of Genesis 24 gave me a new appreciation for the Holy Spirit, and I realized how stingy I had been in saying "Thank You, Lord" for His love gifts.

God Puts the Spotlight on You and Me

God likes us. He loves us. He wants to put the spotlight on you and me and show us off to the heavenly audience, that cloud of witnesses.

Wherefore, seeing we also are compassed about with so great a cloud of witnesses, let us lay aside every weight, and the sin which doth so easily beset us, and let us run with patience the race that is set before us. (Hebrews 12:1)

> *To the intent that now, unto the principalities and powers in heavenly places, might be known by the church the manifold wisdom of God.* (Ephesians 3:10)

No one likes persecution . . . but we all like to go to the movies to watch some hero fight through difficult circumstances because we know that he or she will be vindicated and will become the hero in the end. God has made us to love those kinds of situations. That is part of His character, so that is part of our character. That's why we love to sit there and live out, in our emotions, what is happening on the screen.

In real life we are the real thing. The movies just portray a picture of this principle hidden deep within our spirits by God. This is what we were born for . . . to win. To be the hero, along with our other brother and sister heroes who refused to compromise, but go *after* our predestined plan that God arranged for us. He that is after the flesh is flesh, but he that is *after* the Spirit is spirit. (Romans 8:5)

Our Father loves to watch us come out smelling like a rose. This is real. To win and have a great time doing it is the will of God for us! Sure, it requires fighting! Yes, there is a price to pay. It would be just a cheap, temporary thrill if there were not. It's exciting to win, but you have to expect the punches and keep on going so that you can say, "Hurray! Hallelujah!" in the end. "My God, *I did* it!" He will know that you know you did it with Him as the center of your motivation and your strength.

Paul was a good fighter. He said, *"The Spirit itself beareth witness with our spirit, that we are the children of God; And if children, then heirs—heirs of God, and joint-heirs with Christ—if so be that we suffer with him that we may be also glorified together."* (Romans 8:17) The word glorified mean "put in the spotlight." Just like a hero has spotlights put on him to point him out to the audience, so God wants to put the spotlight on you, so that you can put the spotlight on Him.

Jesus said, *"And now, O Father, glorify thou me now with thine own self with the glory which I had with thee before the world was."* (John 17:5) Jesus was in the spotlight, about to be crucified, and then rise from the dead. He was the star of the show. His motive was that He wanted the world to see how much the Father loved the world that He gave His only beloved Son, but at that moment, Jesus was the one that the world was looking at. He wanted to glorify the Father as the Father glorified Him.

We Are Headed for Glory

We get glorified when the character and the authority of the Lord in us is evident to others and our actions make them look at the Lord. Paul said that we were first foreknown, predestined, called, sanctified, and *glorified* (Romans 8:29,30)

No, we can't take any of the credit for this plan and for our strength to do what the Father has called us to do. And *yes,* we must always be careful to readjust our motives all the time in order to keep from falling into pride. That is essential.

But it is also true that God has called us to victory, and in order to do that we must look ahead to the end of the battle and see the reward. He is our reward. To finally hear His words, *"Well done, thou good and faithful servant"* (Matthew 25:21,23) will be awesome. It is not arrogance to be doing the Father's will, *"That they may see your good works, and glorify your Father who is in heaven."* (Matthew 5:16)

Reject False Pride

Does your ego keep you from allowing someone else to work in the church? Are the gifts only for the ministers, or for all believers? Is your church stifled because you won't allow someone else to do what you haven't learned to do?

You must watch your motives all the time to make sure that you are not doing any of this for self vain-glory. Be ever watchful that this does not happen, and when it does, *as it will,* reject that thought, rebuke it, ask forgiveness for it, and quickly go on to walk in the power of the Lord and expect Him to get the glory from your life as He and only He deserves. You are allowed to enjoy the satisfaction that you are walking in obedience. False pride and false humility both stink. But you don't have to go there if you know God has predestined you for the throne, and that is your only motive!

Motives. Self-worth. Values. Our schools, our psychologists, our parents are always trying to give us self worth. God's idea of your self-worth is that He is not making you figure out how to be a happy human being. He is making you of value to Himself. He is making you *for* Himself. If that is also your goal, then you *will* become happy and motivated and full of self-worth. Not the other way around. He must come first in your life.

He is the reason we eat healthy foods and want to stay strong.

He is the reason we want to be full of love for our neighbor.

He is the reason we want to find a good mate and create children for Him.

He is the reason we want to preach the gospel, heal the sick, cleanse the lepers.

He is the reason we win in the end.

He is the Beginning and the End, the Alpha and the Omega. Read the end of the Book (Revelation 20). We win in the end with Him. Because we allowed Him daily to train us to win here, we will go with him in that day equipped and ready to fight and overcome with Him in the last battle. *"And the armies that were in heaven followed him upon white horses, clothed in fine linen, white and clean. . . . And I saw the beast, and the kings of the earth, and their armies, gathered together to make war against him that sat on the horse and against his army."* (Revelation 19:14,19)

Are you ready, Army ? Are you set, Bride? Go, Mighty Church, in His *name,* the very character and authority of the One who created you to win with Him.

Our motive in serving Jesus is love that shows itself in obedience, but there are going to be incredible rewards given in Heaven for each of us. That will be a wonderful "extra" to anticipate.

Now You Know; Pass It On

Now, pass this truth on to your children. The next generation must be taught, and we cannot wait until the churches get around to telling them.

I once saw an eight year-old deliver several of his friends. I was in New Mexico holding meetings. Ronnie was the pastor's child and had seen and heard deliverance done. As his father and I looked out the window of their house, we saw the boy outside, holding a friend snugly around the middle. The friend was retching.

I've delivered a child as young as four years of age, so don't overlook the youngsters. They can understand more than we give them credit for.

Our youth need to know the truth about power and authority. We would be remiss in our responsibility to them—and in our obedience to God—if we fail in this area. Young people must be taught, shown, encouraged, and helped.

What If We Don't Do It?

If you and I are not willing to follow our Lord Jesus where He calls and do what He says, then we are poorly representing Him. We call ourselves Christians, but does the world see any difference in us? How is it we are being changed from glory unto glory?

Let's Do It

Nowhere in the Bible do we find that God's promises are no longer in effect.

Nowhere in the Bible do we find that Jesus' teaching is no longer in effect.

The early disciples believed what Jesus said—all those incredible, wonderful, challenging things. By the Holy Spirit's power, and full of the authority God gave these men and women, they obeyed.

The Word was true then; and it is true now.

> *And by the hands of the apostles were many signs and wonders wrought among the people (and they were all with one accord in Solomon's porch. And of the rest durst no man join himself to them: but the people magnified them. And believers were the more added to the Lord, multitudes both of men and women), Insomuch that they brought forth the sick into the streets, and laid them on beds and couches, that at the least the shadow of Peter passing by might overshadow some of them.* (Acts 5:12-15)

To Paul, signs and wonders were part of "fully" preaching. *"Through mighty signs and wonders, by the power of the Spirit of God; so that from Jerusalem, and round about unto Illyricum, I have fully preached the gospel of Christ. "* (Romans 15:19)

Eyewitnesses told what they saw; God did the miraculous.

How shall we escape, if we neglect so great salvation, which at the first began to be spoken by the Lord, and was confirmed unto us by them that heard him; God also bearing them witness, both with signs and wonders, and with divers miracles, and gifts of the Holy Ghost, according to his own will? (Hebrews 2:3,4)

Other scriptures confirm the fact of signs and wonders being done: Acts 2:22,43; 4:30; 6:8; 14:3; 15:12; 2 Corinthians 12:12.

And why not? Read these amazing words of Jesus. What power, what authority He entrusted to His followers. Keys of the kingdom. Binding and loosing.

Blessed art thou, Simon Barjona; for flesh and blood hath not revealed it unto thee, but my Father which is in heaven. And I say also unto thee, That thou art Peter, and upon this rock I will build my church, and the gates of hell shall not prevail against it. And I will give unto thee the keys of the kingdom of heaven; and whatsoever thou shalt bind on earth shall be bound in heaven; and whatsoever thou shalt loose on earth shall be loosed in heaven. (Matthew 16:17-19)

Your relationship with God is paramount. If you know Him and love Him, you will naturally want to obey Him.

Let your vision and your testimony be that of Isaiah, *"I saw also the Lord . . . high and lifted up."* Ponder the awesome words of Isaiah 6:1-8). Then ask God what He wants *you* to do.

We're on our way. We're in a battle; we have a job to do. It's power and authority that gets the job done. Obedience is called for. May God work mightily in you, and in us, to His glory. ✝

My prayer for you is the same as Paul's for the church when he prophesied that, *"The God of peace shall bruise Satan under your feet shortly."* (Romans 16:20)

* * *

Notes . . .

Chapter 10

Ready Reference -- HOW TO

This chapter is for all you who have persistently called and written us since our last book *Don't Be Denied God's Power* came out, especially for friends Shirley and Max who are constantly telling me, "Tell us *how* to do it." They don't want to hear generalities; they demand to know, step by step, what to do.

From my experiences of 37 years as a pastor and the seven years since retirement as I continue an active schedule of ministering, healing, and deliverance, here are practical tips and suggestions. Ask God to show you how these can apply to you and your life.

We'll look at three opportunities for ministry. First, healing ourselves and keeping ourselves healthy and strong. Second, healing others. Third, casting spirits out of people.

General Principles for Ministry

1. Expect God to do what He says.

2. Avoid clichés and church doctrine. Keep it simple, as the Bible does.

3. Don't allow yourself to become rushed. Before you start praying for a person, find out either by questions or by the Holy Spirit what the real problem is. It may not be what the person thinks it is. Sometimes it's not healing, but deliverance that he needs.

4. God does not ask you to do something that you can't do.

5. Don't blame the person for the predicament he finds himself in. He probably already feels guilty. Ask the Holy Spirit to give you the words to say.

6. The more you exercise the authority God gives you the more you will have. It's like a muscle to be developed.

7. Don't allow yourself to become discouraged. You do what He says and leave the results with Him.

Healing Yourself

Understand the teaching of body, soul, and spirit. It's by our spirit that we make our bodies obey us. (See Chapter 3)

1.   It is best to keep yourself well and not let an illness get an upper hand. If you've been sick for very long, you may be weakened and not able to do the spiritual warfare by yourself. In that event, call upon a bold believer who knows how to do it.

2.   Know your resources. Have a list of faith-building scriptures at hand. Read them, speak them aloud.

3.   Be willing to obey God. Ask the Holy Spirit for wisdom to find out if there is some matter of obedience. You may be directed to change some dietary or health-related activity. Take that step of obedience.

4.   Determine if this could be a curse handed down from your family line. Cancer "runs" in the family, for example. (See Chapter 7)

5.   Determine if this could be a James curse, which is caused by another Christian. (See Chapteer 7)

6.   Pray boldly, claiming your healing on the basis that your spirit is stronger than your body and your body can be made to obey.

7.   Take your healing. No longer speak of "my" disease. You can describe the symptoms, but do not claim the disease. "I have been healed. Now the symptoms are abating and I am stronger each day."

8.   Speak to your body and tell it to line up with your spirit which agrees with the Word.

9.   If you don't get an instant miracle, then God is going to give you a healing. This takes time.

10.   Sometimes your healing has to be fought for because the enemy doesn't want you well. This involves resisting the symptoms and feelings and knowing that you're entitled to this healing.

Healing Someone Else

1.   Do not rush in to minister healing. Take time to hear from the Spirit. Find out what He wants to do.

2.   You need to determine whether this person needs healing or deliverance.

3.   You may want to ask any unbelieving people to leave the room as Jesus did. (Luke 8:49-56)

4.   It is not in a multitude of prayers that a person is healed. The healing comes as a result of spoken authority.

5. It's not necessary to have a crowd of believers circling the chair where the seeker is sitting. If there are some believers present, then they are instructed to pray silently in agreement.

6. You are the one taking control of the situation, and you will be ministering out loud.

7. Ask the seeker specifically what he or she wants the Lord to do.

8. Ask him if he believes God can do it.

9. Some people throw their healing away because they didn't get an obvious miracle, and their healing is not necessarily felt any more than your stomach would tell you that the pill you just swallowed had gotten there. Even after it does, it still has to get into the bloodstream and go to the problem. Shouldn't we give God the same consideration we give the pill?

10. Ask the person if he believes God is willing to do it, and is He willing to do it now?

11. Ask him if he deserves it.

12. Ask him if God shows him a matter of sin to take care of, or a step of obedience to take, is he willing to do it?

13. Thank God in advance.

14.   Pronounce his healing with the authority Jesus gives you. Now is not the time for a lengthy prayer. Make it short, like Jesus did.

15.   Tell him that not feeling like he is healed has nothing to do with it. The Word says he is healed.

16.   Instruct him that if he's taking medication for the problem, the body will react. He should go to see the physician who prescribed it. Do not instruct the person to discontinue his medication, and avoid giving medical advice.

17.   Be careful not to use the word "counseling" in publicizing or advertising your ministry. Some states regulate the counseling industry, and you could find yourself in trouble with the law.

Delivering Someone

Note: You cannot deliver yourself. This needs to be done by a person who has spiritual authority.

1.   Arrange a time and place where you can concentrate on getting the job done.

2.   Don't accept defeat, or the devils will use it against you next time.

3.   Don't be in a hurry. Find out what you're dealing with before you start speaking. Rushing in too soon brings doubt and defeat.

4.   Do not gather a group around you. One, or at the most, several people can be there, and their job is to intercede silently in agreement with you.

5.   You do the speaking; you take charge of the deliverance.

6.   You do not need to ask the person about all of his/her past sins or what has led to him to being in this condition. You need only a minimum of information. Do not let him talk on and on.

7.   Find out if he is a Christian. If not, lead him to salvation because there is nothing to keep the demonic out unless he has accepted the Lord.

8.   Establish for him your authority in Christ to do this deliverance.

9.   If he shies from the word "demon," you may use the term "spirits" or "fallen angels."

10.   The person being delivered should not attempt to "help" in any way. This means he should be quiet, not pray or speak in tongues.

11.   Some of the results of the deliverance may not be apparent instantly.

12. Healing needs to be administered to the place where the demons have previously resided.

13. Instruct the person how to maintain his freedom. He or she must speak aloud to cast it out when demons try to harass them in the future. Pray for him to be filled with the Holy Spirit. ✝

* * *

Let's Get Personal

"All of this looks so difficult. Is this really what I have to do?"

Ask most people what it means to be a "good" Christian. You'll hear such things as: go to church, give your money when the plate is passed, and treat people with love. We have had an incomplete and incorrect view of what a Christian is and does. For years we've imagined that God is going to be very forgiving so we can do whatever comes our way.

At the other extreme, deep down in our hearts, we've feared finding out the truth. We're sure we can never really measure up.

The truth is in the Word. We read it like we're skimming the phone book, looking for a particular number. Slow down, read it like you were there, seeing the events unfold right before you.

The truth is there. Grace, Love, Salvation. And healing and deliverance. Ask the Holy Spirit to show you.

Take a few minutes to identify the hindrances and roadblocks the devil has set in your way to trip you up. You can cry, moan, murmur, and complain about it, but view these aggravations God's way, as hurdles. When you leap over them by the power of the Holy Spirit, you gain new strength, new authority.

Be honest as you complete these sentences.

1. My relationship with God right now is - - -

2. My prayer life, right now, is - - -

3. My reading of the Bible is - - -

4. Faulty teaching and faulty perceptions about God -

5. What I want to do with the rest of my life - - -

6 What I plan to do first - - -

7. My unresolved wounds are - - -

- • Memories of my parents - - -

- • Memories of my childhood - - -

- • My siblings - - -

- • My spouse - - -

- • People at the churches I used to attend - - -

- • My school experiences - - -

I can do all things through Christ who strengtheneth me. (Philippians 4:13)

Are you ready? Make a gentle start, step out by faith, and take God at His Word.

Healing and deliverance are not the exclusive domain of a paid, professional clergy or traveling evangelists and "healers." God has called each one of us to a life of obedience. You can reach people who wouldn't go to church or a special meeting.

This means that instead of reading about it, thinking about it, worrying about it, wondering about it, you actually begin to *do* it. Use the power and authority God wants you to have. ✝

* * *

Introducing Stan Riley

Stan Riley does what he talks about. With a ready smile he reaches for his old, worn Bible to show you what God says.

Born in Canada, Stan brought his wife, Millie, and youngsters to Prescott, Arizona years ago. Successful in his career, he tells you he was an unlikely candidate to be a pastor. Yet he relates how a man on the construction job kept pestering him to go to visit his church. Finally Stan said he would, and made the mistake of telling his wife and young son, Jimmy. That Sunday Jimmy came to the breakfast table all dressed up, ready to go. Stan was annoyed and told the youngster that he didn't mean to go today. But within the hour the two were entering the church building. Jimmy paraded clear down to the front row. A message was given; Stan can't recall the words, he just remembers the response of his heart. Born again, Stan went down the block the next week to buttonhole all the neighbors about this wonderful new life in Christ.

Eventually Stan started a church, Mountain Fellowship. He taught classes at Scottsdale Community College. He ministered healing and deliverance weekly. He wrote several books, the best known being *Don't Be Denied God's Power.*

His speaking has taken him to Canada, New Mexico, Kansas City, Colorado, California, Montana, Wyoming, Hawaii, and Texas. He spoke once at the largest Catholic church in Amarillo, Texas. At Taos, New Mexico, he ministered for a week with a team at a large hippie commune. Such denominations as Methodist, Assembly of God, Catholic, Foursquare, and Presbyterian have welcomed him in the pulpit.

After 37 years of full-time ministry, which included three speaking trips to Nigeria, he felt ready to retire. God had other plans, however. He brought Marilee into Stan's life after the death of Millie. Together they maintain a very active schedule of personal ministry for those who phone, invite them over, or show up on their doorstep. Stan has appeared on TV. His book, *Don't Be Denied God's Power,* has gone around the world. In December of 1999, the Lord gave Stan a powerful prophetic word for those in leadership. Over 500 copies of this letter went to key pastors and the leadership of parachurch organizations in the U.S. and several foreign nations.

Stan intends this book to bring all of us up to speed so we can bring glory to God.

If it sparks a renewal in your life, or if it raises more questions, the Rileys would like to hear from you.

* * *

Renewal Ministries
P. O. Box 913
Prescott, Arizona 86302

Don't Be Denied God's Power
by Stan Riley

The Christian Church as a whole, needs to take a fresh look at itself and begin to question its apparent complacency toward spiritual power.

This book will attempt to:

1) explain, define, and expose Satan's devices against the Church and its people

2) answer your questions by giving experiences of deliverances

3) show you how many ministries have been destroyed by Satan's intricately designed and planned traps.
Satan will try any deception to ruin any one of God's servants and keep children of God from overcoming and obtaining eternal life.

Notes . . .

Notes . . .

Notes . . .